NIGHT ERRANDS

NIGHT

How Poets Use Dreams

ERRANDS

EDITED BY

Roderick Townley

University of Pittsburgh Press

Published by the University of Pittsburgh Press, Pittsburgh, Pa. 15261
Copyright © 1998, Roderick Townley
All rights reserved
Manufactured in the United States of America
Printed on acid-free paper
10 9 8 7 6 5 4 3 2 1

Library of Congress Cataloging-in-Publication Data and
acknowledgments of permissions will be found at the end of this book.

A CIP catalog record for this book is available from the
British Library.

To Paul Fussell
for his wit, friendship, and
inexcusable good cheer

Dig deeper, mon ami, *the rock maidens*
are running naked in the dark cellars.

William Carlos Williams

CONTENTS

Acknowledgments   xi

Introduction   1

Deciphering the Dream: The Day Logic of Poetic Process   13
LAUREL BLOSSOM

On the Past, Poetry, and Dream   24
MICHAEL BURNS

Out of the Underworld: Poetry and Dreams   28
NICHOLAS CHRISTOPHER

Impressionism and the Army Corps of Engineers   39
SARAH COTTERILL

Poems and Dreams   44
RACHEL HADAS

Missing the Boat   51
ANTHONY HECHT

Sleeplessness   57
EDWARD HIRSCH

The Dream of the Trumpeter   64
JOHN HOLLANDER

The Dream and the Bagel   74
DAVID IGNATOW

Seventeen Arcana from the Infinity of Dreams   78
ROBERT KELLY

Inside Out   87
FAYE KICKNOSWAY

Scrubbed Up and Sent to School   97
MAXINE KUMIN

Interweavings: Reflections on the Role of Dream
in the Making of Poems   105
DENISE LEVERTOV

Dream Song   120
PHILIP LEVINE

The Stuff That Dreams Are Made Of   129
GERARD MALANGA

Dream Scripts   133
PAUL MARIANI

Some Footnotes to My Dreams   144
J. D. McCLATCHY

Dark Dreams, Dark Sayings: Poems About Trauma   154
WESLEY McNAIR

"Nostalgia": Dream, Memory, Poetry   162
JOYCE CAROL OATES

Dreamwork, Griefwork, Poemwork   170
DAVID RAY

The Unremembered Dream   181
PATRICIA TRAXLER

How My Green Silk Dreams
Led to the Concept of Personal Mythology   186
DIANE WAKOSKI

One Hand on the Pen, One in the Dream   194
JANE O. WAYNE

Remembering "Caliban Remembers"   200
THEODORE WEISS

A Note on Poetry and Dreams   226
RICHARD WILBUR

A Resource of Dreaming   234
ROBLEY WILSON

Selected Bibliography   239

ACKNOWLEDGMENTS

I have many people to thank for help with this project. Rachel Hadas, one of the first poets to sign on, provided encouragement and invaluable contacts. Richard Howard gave wise and early counsel. Cynthia Miller of the University of Pittsburgh Press provided enthusiastic support throughout the book's long gestation. My appreciation, as well, to all the poets who contributed to *Night Errands*. A special thanks is due those who signed on before there was a publisher in sight. They include, beside Rachel Hadas: Sarah Cotterill, Anthony Hecht, John Hollander, David Ignatow, Faye Kicknosway, Maxine Kumin, Denise Levertov, J. D. McClatchy, Joyce Carol Oates, David Ray, Patricia Traxler, Jane O. Wayne, and Theodore Weiss. As for the poets who expressed a desire to contribute to the book but found themselves overcommitted to other projects, I must accept their good wishes in lieu of essays.

I've benefited as well from scholarly advice. Professor Joan Fillmore Hooker provided important hints about T. S. Eliot; Paul Mariani illuminated for me the dreams of Robert Lowell and John Berryman; and Judith Moffett helped steer me though recent James Merrill scholarship. My thanks to John Weisman, Stephen Dickman, and Peter Manning for their bright minds and lifelong friendship; to Joanne and Russell Baker for their unfailing support; to Michael F. Hunt for calls out of the blue; and to Gloria Vando and Bill Hickok for welcoming us on our arrival in Kansas City and providing helpful contacts. Finally, all thanks to my wife, Wyatt: my joy, support, and in-house editor extraordinaire.

NIGHT ERRANDS

INTRODUCTION

"The dream is an involuntary kind of poetry," wrote British psychologist Charles Rycroft. The reverse is true as well, of course. Poetry is a hard-won kind of dream. Both are suffused with a doubleness, or ambiguity, that quickly evaporates under the glare of paraphrase. Both employ compression and startling imagery and proceed by leaps rather than conventional logic. Most basically, both are forms of play.

"Play," in this context, stands for open-ended thought, rather than closed, punchline-producing, problem-solving cerebration. Liam Hudson has written a remarkable book called *Night Life: The Interpretation of Dreams*, in which he describes open-ended thought "in terms of those reveries, free associations and fantasies in which there is no regulative intention, and no attempt is made to follow a train or sequence through to a conclusion. In practice, it contributes to the solution of tightly knit problems, in that it provides the raw material for what Einstein and others have referred to as associative or combinatory play."

This suggests another connection. "Dreaming," declares Richard M. Jones in *The Dream Poet*, "is a form of thinking experienced as action." So is poetry. A poem does not lie on the page, it zithers down it like a spooked garter snake. We need to turn our popular concepts on their heads: Dreams are not the product of inactivity, and poems are not for the passive. Poetry is the most athletic form of literature.

There are, of course, poets who have not relied on dream, even some great ones, such as the author of *The Dunciad* and *An Essay on Criticism*. True, Pope lived in the Age of Reason, not the Realm of Dream. It was a strangely fragile Lockian time capsule in which logic, hierarchy, satire, and wit were supremely valued, and the intuitive largely ignored.

It may also be true that more poets went berserk during the oneirically deprived eighteenth century than at any time before or since.

In our own time, there are poets who appear not to have been sourced by dream, just as there are plants that live on air alone, with no roots reaching into the ground. Such poetry is a "conscious product shaped and designed to have the effect intended," as Jung declared in a 1922 lecture, "On the Relation of Analytical Psychology to Poetry." Works of this kind, he says, fine as they may be, "nowhere overstep the limits of comprehension."

But there are other poetries, relying to a greater or lesser extent on the unconscious. At the far extreme are works that "positively force themselves upon the author," declares Jung. "His hand is seized, his pen writes things that his mind contemplates with amazement." With such poems, he says, "we would expect a strangeness of form and content, thoughts that can only be apprehended intuitively, a language pregnant with meanings, and images that are true symbols because they are the best possible expressions for something unknown—bridges thrown out towards an unseen shore."

The poets represented in this volume understand the generative relationship between dreams and poems. Some—like the late David Ignatow—modify the definition of dreams to include creative revery; but all recognize the importance of unconscious sources, however they are tapped. This recognition cuts across all styles and schools. Indeed, the intention has been to include poets of all aesthetic stripes—committed formalists, devotees of Olson and Williams, New York Schoolers, wild surrealists, and others. A wide age range is represented, from poets in their forties, still solidifying their reputations, to elders in their seventies and eighties, garlanded with honors. But they are united in their lively engagement with the topic of dreams. Even Edward Hirsch, who has contributed a sort of counter-essay in praise of insomnia, celebrates the "obscure underground thinking" that leads to "poetic fluency." It is as if these poets have been just *waiting* for someone to ask them to write about the subject.

Among the most intriguing dreams are those which poets have about other poets. Such dreams tend to be consolatory—Rachel Hadas, for instance, dreaming about the recently departed James Merrill; or Denise Levertov dreaming about Robert Duncan, with whom she'd had a falling out before his final illness. But literary dreams are not always so benign. One well-known poet, having completed his first book-length poem, had a dream "in which some older man with a bulging brow and a spindly body, looking much like Allen Tate, was saying louringly, 'You are not *important* enough to write poems like that!'" Then there is Elizabeth Bishop's dream argument with George Herbert about whether Marianne Moore's meter was superior to John Donne's. The two finally agreed that Moore was better than Donne, but not quite up to Herbert himself. "This may have been subconscious politeness on my part," Bishop jotted in her notebook afterward.

One wonders what Freud would have made of all this. In an early formulation, the father of dream analysis propounded the idea that the mind thinks in two distinct modes: "primary processes," which characterize dreams, neuroses, and infancy; and "secondary processes," which take charge of normal waking life. These modes he considered antithetical. The dreamworld, realm of the id, seemed to him a cauldron: "It is filled with energy reaching it from the instincts, but it has no organization," he wrote. "The logical laws of thought do not apply . . . [and] contrary impulses exist side by side without canceling each other out." The waking mind, on the other hand—realm of the ego—is verbal, rational, chronological, categorical. To think in the second mode is to repress the first.

Psychoanalyst Charles Rycroft properly dismisses the Freudian dichotomy as fallacious and, in his brilliant work *The Innocence of Dreams*, identifies many connections between "primary" and "secondary" thought patterns. If Freud had lived today, he suggests, he would have seen the connections himself and worked to translate what Rycroft calls "oneiric, iconic utterances [dream thinking] into verbal, phonetic statements [the waking mode]." In practice, this is what poets do all the time. They have learned the art of sleeping with one eye open, taking the charged imagery of the subconscious and shaping it into art. The trick is to balance the two modes: immerse oneself in the subconscious, then reassert the intellect to shape the result.

Actually the process is practically simultaneous—the two modes of thought constantly feeding lines to each other. Not every poet gets the balance right. As T. S. Eliot drily observed: "The bad poet is usually unconscious where he ought to be conscious, and conscious where he ought to be unconscious." *Night Errands* contains the thinking of over two dozen contemporary American poets on the role of the unconscious in literature. These poets know they do not stand alone but continue to learn from their predecessors, whose pioneering use of dream materials and other resources helped give twentieth-century poetry its direction.

For many of us, contemporary poetry starts with William Carlos Williams. His "broken / pieces of a green / bottle" and other spiky imagery suggest a commitment to the outer rather than the inner world, to reality rather than dream, until one realizes that reality and dream are not opposites, and that dream images have nothing "dreamy" about them. In fact, they have a super- or *sur*-reality. So it is that Williams could argue that "Works of art . . . must be real, not 'realism' but reality itself," and at the same time declare, with no inconsistency, "The poem is a dream."

Williams was a busy doctor, a man of logic and practicality, who yet was able to dive within himself, sometimes between one patient and the next, and come up with glinting shards of poetry. He understood that form devoid of a strong subterranean impulse is sterile, and that impulse without form is just bad poetry. The results were uneven; but at his best he was able to bring conscious and unconscious together and make form *instinctive*.

For Williams it had to be "organic" form. He declared the sonnet dead—in part, one is tempted to say, because he could not write a decent one, but also because of his notion of "contact." It was not his way to fashion a silver cage, lower it on a silken string into the subconscious, and hope to catch something. For Williams, the form of the poem had to *grow out of* the subject—and out of the spoken language—as the torsion of a shell grows out of the necessities of a sea creature's life. At his most interesting, particularly in the prose-poem sequence *Kora in Hell: Improvisations*, Williams writes the way dreams move, by juxtaposition and compression. He learned these devices from the cubist and surrealist artists he admired, as well as from observing the motions of his own mind.

Another master of juxtaposition was Williams's old nemesis, T. S. Eliot. Eliot's poetry, as critic Joan Fillmore Hooker observes, is "drenched in allusions to dreams." She cites his "mosaic or juxtapositional style, leaving out the connections, as dreams do." In "The Waste Land," Eliot creates a sort of sonic collage in which voices emerge from the general welter: music hall ditties, bits of old plays, snatches of conversation overheard in Dante's hell.

Occasionally, from references in Eliot's letters, we learn that a particular image came from a dream (the sinuous line in "Animula": "Pray for Floret, by the boarhound slain between the yew trees," for example). But whether Eliot is mining or merely miming actual dreams is seldom clear. Ronald Bush's essential book, *T. S. Eliot: A Study in Character and Style*, suggests that for Eliot dreams are an intensified form of drama. Bush writes: "Since they provide unexplained particulars charged with emotion from below, and are thus more authentically involved with our buried lives, dreams give the prototype for lyric poetry."

What concerned Eliot, as much as the structural scheme of "The

Waste Land," was the creation of a charged atmosphere, or dominant tone. This hypnotic quality unifies the poem's details, just as our dreams give cohesiveness to the most disparate events and images. Under its spell, as Eliot remarked in another context, even a nonsense rhyme (on the order of "Here we go round the prickly pear") can seem "a tremendous statement, like statements made in our dreams."

If Williams looked to dreams for clues to poetic structure, and Eliot for tone and archetype, many of the poets following them, from the late 1940s onward, rummaged through dreams for more autobiographical materials. The term *confessional poets*, of course, is misleading. Robert Lowell, Anne Sexton, John Berryman, Sylvia Plath, and others wrote in differing styles and were concerned about many subjects besides their own maladjustments. Nonetheless, there is an emphasis on anguished personal experience that is different from what came before. In "Last Night" in the volume *History*, Robert Lowell recounts—as if for an analyst—a dream of his own death:

> I opened an old closet door, and found myself
> covered with quicklime, my face deliquescent . . .
> by oversight still recognizable.
> Thank God, I was the first to find myself . . .

Lowell's recent biographer, the poet/critic Paul Mariani, finds that many of the later poems, particularly those in *Day by Day*, "slide between waking and sleeping, and give us a sense of a somnambulist."

Mariani has also written a biography of John Berryman, and in a recent letter confirms that "the evidence of dreams is everywhere" in Berryman's work. "In fact, he spent the year before writing his *Dream Songs* writing long psychological explanations of his dreams, parsing them, unraveling layer on layer of them, watching for puns and double entendres." In many of these "songs," Mariani continues, Berryman relayed his dreams "in a dreamlike manner, uninhibited, the sentence cut to its essentials, puns galore, and weird, wild humor." His poem "Dream Song No. 327" is actually about Freud's dream theories, and ends:

> I tell you, Sir, you have enlightened but
> you have misled us: a dream is a panorama
> of the whole mental life,
> I took one once to forty-three structures, that
> accounted in each for each word: I did not yell "mama"
> nor did I take it out on my wife.

Forty-three structures? Even allowing for exaggeration, that is a major investment in nocturnal research.

Anne Sexton, too, was deeply involved in dream analysis, often with the help of a therapist. One of Sexton's biographers, Diane Wood Middlebrook, attempting to characterize the poet's techniques, points to the "associational forays that do not develop into thoughts but terminate in surreal images." This is the path dreams take as well, whether daydreams or night dreams. "I had a dream last night," writes Sexton in "Consorting with Angels":

> Adam was on the left of me
> and Eve was on the right of me,
> both thoroughly inconsistent with the world of reason.
> We wove our arms together
> and rode under the sun.
> I was not a woman anymore,
> not one thing or the other.

The relief of escaping from the labels we are known by—of not having to be, for a while, "one thing or the other"—surely this is one of the gifts of dream, as it is of the related realms of fantasy, intuition, and myth.

One of the greatest escape artists of our time, aesthetically speaking, was James Merrill. For this uncategorizable poet, at once traditionalist and iconoclast, dreams were a major resource. A close friend, J. D. McClatchy, reports that Merrill "used to keep *The Oxford Book of Dreams* right by the john! And often transcribed his dreams into his notebooks."

The much anthologized "The Mad Scene" begins: "Again last night I dreamed the dream called Laundry"; and there are others— "Dreams of Clothes," for instance—in which dream materials are overt. More often, though, Merrill's dreams remain unnamed sources, like the informant Deep Throat in a D.C. garage, never revealing their identity. An extraordinary glimpse into these covert operations is found in *The Emerging Goddess: The Creative Process in Art, Science, and Other Fields*, by Albert Rothenberg, M.D., who was for a time Merrill's analyst. Rothenberg does not mention the poet by name but devotes a hundred closely printed pages to a discussion of Merrill's "In Monument Valley."

Evidently, the poem originated in a picnic with a friend among the rock formations of Monument Valley, Arizona. A sandstorm blew up and suddenly a bedraggled horse, near starvation, appeared before them. Merrill later drafted a poem about the horse. With a rough first draft on the page, the poet slept and had two dreams, neither of which seemed related to the poem, since both had mostly indoor settings and involved his mother and grandmother. But Rothenberg shows that the dreams were *structurally* related to the developing poem and contained oedipal elements that Merrill would confront in the next draft. Merrill then had a third dream, his description of which was duly tape-recorded by the doctor:

> I may be going to Brazil again. . . . Elizabeth Bishop needs a doctor, her hands are covered with scabs and scales. She tells me that Marianne Moore is getting married to a much younger man. Now we glimpse Marianne Moore gallantly descending alone into a New York subway. The map of Brazil, retraced and colored, becomes the face and shoulders of an old woman wearing a cardigan. A telephone call. The trip is off.

The next day, Merrill rewrote his poem from the beginning. Whatever the meaning of the dream, it clearly freed up unconscious materials and helped him push his poem forward.

"Meaning" is seldom a straightforward matter when it comes to dreams. Their imagery, like poetry's, can suggest several things at once, offering what Pound calls "an intellectual and emotional complex in an instant of time." But the relationship of dream to poem goes deeper than imagery. In fact, the three dreams that proved so helpful to Merrill contain *none* of the images that appear in the final poem—no horse, no desert, no rock—suggesting there are ways of using dreams that go beyond the pilfering of images.

Simply carting the furniture of a dream over to a poem is not, in itself, going to make the poem deep. James Tate, in fact, thinks it is a bad idea to try to recapture a dream and says he never does it, although his poetry has been described as dreamlike or surrealistic. "When you're in a waking state trying to capture a dream," Tate remarked recently, "you're in a process of losing things. It's not a process of discovery, although you may think it is. If you go chasing after a dream you're going to get lost. You're *full* of these fragments of dreams anyway. They'll find *you*."

It is essential to avoid thinking of such fragments as raw materials. The landscape of dream is not just one more natural resource to be strip-mined and left exposed to sunlight. We are speaking about the deepest parts of ourselves, and anything taken from that land deserves to be handled with reverence. As poet David Ray observes: "The poem is altar for the dream."

How to approach this altar? Tate says he likes to give himself a good three hours per writing session. The first hour or two involves forgetting. Really, the process mimics falling asleep. Only after the mow-the-lawn and pay-the-mortgage details have drained from the mind can one hope to reach the deeper currents where words come alive. This is what Tate calls the leaping off point, the doorway into the poem.

The country that lies on the other side of this doorway is much like the landscape of dream, a land of free association and startling images where (to recall Freud's words about the subconscious) "contrary impulses exist side by side without canceling each other out." No surprise, then, that poetic revery so often jumps the stiles of logic separating field from field and grazes among ambiguities.

One hears complaints about ambiguity from those who value the straightforward. What does it all *mean*? Why can't poets say what they *mean*? Often, there is something legitimate about the public's irritation with contemporary poetry. A lot of facile surrealism poses as profundity, and it is not always easy to distinguish willful obscurity from the inevitable ambiguity of deep imagery. Actually, the best poets are always hunting down the exact word, the precise phrase, firing off panicky letters to editors to be *sure* that a semi-colon has been changed to a comma. Confusion is the last thing they want; it would defeat the whole enterprise, which is communication, from deep to deep.

All this takes a special kind of bravery, a willingness to enter the dark wood of the subconscious and confront whatever lives there. Unlike the knights errant of the past, who merely slew their dragons and brought back their bloody tongues, the poet's night errand is to bring his creature back alive, its tongue intact and singing. The songs will be enigmatic, even after the poet has given them form and translated them into the waking vernacular. The strangeness is still upon them. That's what makes them poetry.

And so, although poets shun obscurity, they embrace ambiguity—seeing around corners, hearing contrary truths without tuning any of them out. In this sense, ambiguity is clarity; linear thinking is confusion. As Hudson observes: "In the hands of the sufficiently skilled, ambiguity is a property of words that gives us access to just those recesses of experience that other modes of expression fail to reach."

There have always been opposing ways of knowing the world. One goes back to Rilke and Gide, specifically to the image of Gide picking up a little glass giraffe from a desk and examining it with a scientist's intensity until he has grasped everything about it, from the craftsmanship to the materials that went into it. But Rilke? One critic writes: "To understand a thing deeply, Rilke would close his eyes."

This is why poets are our designated dreamers. They are the ones we count on to drive us home at the end of the party, after our logicians, accountants, analysts, anatomists have broken the china, lied about statistics, and made passes at the professor's wife. Because it is the poets, finally, who know where we live. They know the dark house at the end of the cul-de-sac.

At the heart of the poetic enterprise is a radical assumption: that the right-angled thinking which has built our great cities and invented television and the rest is a severely limited thinking. Not wrong or bad, but limited. The artist is receptive to at least two modes of thinking at once and is able, in Rycroft's words, to "oscillate between active and passive states of being, and between objectivity and subjectivity, without feeling that [his] identity is threatened by doing so." The self that creates art, he continues, "is not the 'I' or Ego that opposes itself to the rest of the universe, but some wider, less personal self to which the 'I' has to abandon itself, in the case of dreaming by falling asleep, in the case of waking imaginative activity by attainment of that receptive state of mind which Keats called Negative Capability." Depending on the kind of poet one is, this expanded self could be the primeval morass of preconscious existence or the realm of spirit. For mystical poets (there still are some), dreams and visions of the night are meant to instruct us, and the poem that results is an instrument of healing.

Healing the split within us after a lifetime of internal exile— therein lies the secret lure of poetry. It is a lure that our egos are anxious to resist. Hudson puts the matter well. The average educated reader, he writes, "is anchored in the prosaic. Even if he is beguiled briefly, it is to the bedrock of common sense that he returns. The poet's task . . . is not

. . . to release him on a brief flight of fancy that leaves his prosaic under-standing intact. It is to destabilise that prosaic understanding, and replace it with one that is deeper."

Figuring out the literal message of a poem, then, is as unproduc-tive as figuring out a dream. "Almost everyone wants interpretations *instead* of the dream," remarked W. S. Merwin in a recent letter. "I want the dreams to continue to well up out of themselves, which means to a great degree in their own terms. So the powerful ones remain insofar as possible objects of contemplation more than of analysis. A dream is a glimpse of a dimension, and translating it is like saying of a poem, 'In other words, you mean . . .'"

The artist hopes to outwit literal thinking by casting spells that make our logical heads spin. Formal rituals (the poet's bag of tricks) establish a sense of impending magic (Eliot's dominant tone); and deeply resonant images create what Hudson calls "inexplicit tensions . . . unre-solvable but contained." Such images, often originating in dream, point in all directions at once, foiling interpretation.

It is a rare moment when a poet is given the grace of such a cre-ation, a poem so magnetized by invisible forces that readers return to it again and again, anxious to fall under its spell once more. Like Rilke's famous torso of Apollo, such writing breaks out

> of all its contours
> like a star: for there is no place
> that does not see you. You must change your life.

LAUREL BLOSSOM

Laurel Blossom has published several volumes,
including *Any Minute* (1979), *What's Wrong*
(1987), and *The Papers Said* (1993). Fellowships
have come her way from the Ohio Arts Council,
the New York Foundation for the Arts, and the
National Endowment for the Arts. Blossom lives in
New York City and is cofounder of The Writers
Community, which is now a part of the YMCA
National Writer's Voice.

DECIPHERING THE DREAM
The Day Logic of Poetic Process

Katie jumped into the ocean blue.
She didn't know how to swim.
The water was murky. I couldn't see.
I was calling her name.

The water cleared. Of a swimming pool
She was lying in the deep deep end.
I held my breath. I dove straight down
To save my childhood friend.

The closer I got to the bottom
The more Katie looked like me.
I took her in my arms
And came back up quickly.

She opened her eyes and stretched and smiled
As I laid her out on the ground.
It's only a dream, she told me.
I never really drowned.

We jumped back into the ocean.
I taught her how to swim.
The seagulls squawked, the dolphins danced,
The world spilled over the brim.

That's the kind of dream I like. Logical, easy to interpret, no loose ends. I suppose, despite my intellectual pretensions and literary ambitions, that's the kind of poem I like too.

Direct access to one's dreams can occur in various ways. The poem above is called "Now We Are 48," and it reproduces the actual progress of a dream, remembered in sharp detail the following morning. Clarity of that kind is rare, however—at least for me. More often, I've had the experience of feeling as if I were taking dictation, which is akin to dreaming, only in words instead of pictures; and I once dreamed the last sentence of a speech I'd been struggling to get right for three solid days and nights.

In between, I've experimented occasionally with automatic writing. A few of the resulting poems I liked well enough to include in my book *The Papers Said,* but they remain atypical. I envy those who can do such poems authentically. My own usual method is more painstaking, more drip than flow, more stalactite or Chinese torture; I want to know—or be able, with some mental exercise, research, or leap of imagination, to discern—the waking connections through which a poem moves. Poems may begin in the subconscious, but they are finished by conscious craft. I am of the school that a poem gets made.

Nevertheless, I think the process of writing a poem, if not like dreaming itself, is very much like deciphering a dream. You may just be able to distinguish the poem's potential shape in the darkness; you may have a word, a phrase, or an image as a clue. To "retrieve" the poem, you must try to follow where the words and images lead, the way you follow the numbers in a connect-the-dots drawing. To take a frivolous example, the flat "a" of "Kansas" in the opening lines of the poem "Doomed" offered a chance to poke fun at my Midwestern accent (and provide information about the woman in the poem):

> The roadsign reads Kansas, another example
> of language imitating life. The land's so flat
> the wind acts as if it would like to blow you to hell . . .

where the assonance enacts and reenacts the landscape (there it goes again) the poem is passing through.

The strategy of another poem, "No Is the Answer, The Answer

Is No," comes from trying to describe what the word *No* feels like and where it leads:

> Then your shoulder or your head or your whole body
> collides with a wall of bricks, the pain
> so dazzling the remotest memories of your childhood
> flare up like faces
>
> when a match is struck in the dark, a glimpse
> of your own quick shadow on the cave wall
> and all the names you call out to come back, come back
> hollow, the smell of sulphur on their breath . . .

The word "No" in the title hits the poem like a bomb. You know how pain can explode behind the eyes like light, suddenly, momentarily, blindingly. Rejection explodes that same way in the poem, illuminating previous rejections like cave paintings on the walls of the mind. Miserable and deluded like the inhabitants of Plato's cave, who saw only shadows and thought them reality, the poem cries out in protest, or need, or self-pity; but all it gets back is an echo, its own emptiness, bitter breath smelling of the devil and rotten eggs.

> or else
>
> a door opens and you rush in, so surprised
> by your forward momentum you wince
> to find yourself intact and standing
> in the room you wanted so badly to stand in—
>
> empty, bare white, no windows, no secrets,
> two doors and a ladderback chair with a rush seat
> planted in the middle of the floor. *This is your life.*
> It makes you want to throw up. The door
>
> back to where you came from stands open, darkness
> hot in your face, somebody laughing, a whole history of failure
> you'd really rather not include in this story.
> *Do you know who that voice is?*

The empty white room feels like a spotlight or like the 1950s TV show *This Is Your Life*, in which some poor celebrity was subjected to embarrassing surprise appearances by old teachers, siblings unseen—and unmourned—for thirty years, and so on, whose voices from backstage had to be guessed at.

> *Do you know who that voice is?* Old flame
>
> Mr. Muse, Sinatra-smooth, two cigarettes in an ashtray
> burning, tempting you
> to confuse the messenger with the message
> it takes a lifetime
>
> to translate into usable language: Shoot.
> Take a shit. Take voice. Take flying lessons.
> Say slough of despond twice with a straight face.
> Write rhymed verse
>
> so accessible it makes you suspect
> among poets and petlovers alike. Relax
> in the lonely chair your father left you,
> the needlepoint chair handed down to you by your mother,
>
> the crooked chair van Gogh painted of himself
> when he was almost happy. These are your instruments
> of torture and deliverance, your Book of Kells, the skeleton
> key in the heart-shaped lock. Twist it
>
> however you like, it opens. You cannot escape
> your freedom.

The poem mocks its own desires and longings, but it knows also that they are the means of its salvation. As in a dream, there are several things going on in the poem at once.

Sometimes these goings-on can be tracked along a string of sound, as with the "a" of "Kansas" in "Doomed," or here, along the "l" beads. "Kells" brought "skeleton" to mind as I was listening for what came next. "Skeleton" led to lock and key, which led to the idea of escape, which led to an insight into the paradoxical desire to escape one's

> . . . freedom. That second door might still, don't you think,
> lead to an absolutely sunstruck patio, fragrant mountains
> by the sea, red geraniums—look! the light

> is bulging at the door,
> longing to engulf you and carry you away
> to *heaven, I'm in heaven,* like poor old, dear old
> dead Fred Astaire, dancing up and down the rungs of his chair.

The second door, mentioned earlier in the poem, could not be abandoned or ignored; it was a problem the poem had to solve, like the proverbial gun in the play's first act. It took a long time and many tries to discover the link forged here, where the door looks as if it leads to freedom but turns out instead to lead to freedom from freedom, a dream of immortality that can only be entered through death.

"No Is the Answer, The Answer Is No" is a good example of the fact that twentieth-century poems proceed, like dreams and psychotherapy, by association. A word leaps to an image, or an image to a word, which leaps by sound or unconscious design to another word or image, so that the poem is a process of discovery, as surprising to the poet as to the reader. If it isn't, if it doesn't create itself the way a dream does as it proceeds, if its path and destination are previously determined, it's DOA, dead on arrival, and no good to anybody, poet and petlover alike.

That's why a poem can take so long, exploring every path to its logical conclusion or dead end. "No Is the Answer, The Answer Is No" took twelve years and forty-odd drafts to finish. Any number of times in the process of writing the poem, I got stuck. For hours, days, weeks, or months I would put the poem aside or try to push it forward. Some of the pieces that got written while I did this I liked and wanted to keep: the Fred Astaire image, for instance, came early. Later I would have to graft those pieces to the main trunk of the poem. I didn't (don't) always succeed. There are still arbitrary transitions, little failures of imagination, bumps. Something more could have happened, I think, in the comparison between poets and petlovers, for instance; the poem moves too abruptly, impatiently, to the admonition "Relax." I want to pause at that juncture, when I read it, and reconsider, as if I've come upon a little gully I have to cross and I know I'm going to get my feet cold and wet.

At such places in the process of writing I try to lie down. My friend Cheri, if awakened, even for some considerable period of time, can fall back asleep and reenter her dreams. I find this a remarkable ability in night dreams. I can't do it. Yet it is exactly what I do when I'm revising or trying to move a poem past a pocket of resistance. I have to go back into the experience of the poem, into the feeling from which the poem arose, into the dream I was dreaming when I first felt the urge to fix it in words.

"The Spin of the Earth" describes the anomalous minute inserted by international agreement between the year gone by and the year upcoming that's necessary every few years to bring our clocks back into alignment with the actual relationship of the earth's rotation to its progress around the sun.

> The timekeepers have their troubles too, probably,
> problems with the wife, the usual fights
> about who's going to feed the research animals
> and what time one should arrive at a party scheduled
> to begin at eight. Especially when it's the new year
>
> that torture, barbarian
> hordes overrunning the known world, and what you do after
> you've bartered your last watch.

The poem got stuck here, as it says it does. I could have taken a cue from "watch" and moved directly to

> It isn't the end of the world, Marion's saying.

—which begins the next stanza. But that would have glossed over the issue. I hadn't gotten to the heart of what constituted the "torture." I was in Rome with the Visigoths, I was with the timekeeper in some Arabian souk where he has had to give up all his modern means of telling time, of keeping track; but I wasn't dead yet. What was the feeling that falling through the cracks of time had given me of danger, of disappearing? What had it reminded me of?

You'd think it would be easy to remember, but it's not, no easier than to recover a dream after you completely wake up. Unless you're Cheri, you have to reinvent the halfway place where you're still in the dream but you're outside it too. You have to induce a kind of objective trance.

I do it by repeating the poem. I repeat it over and over again, either aloud or in my mind—aloud is best—and wait each time when I reach the stuck place to see what spills out. There is often interference, distraction, some other agenda operating. So I get this far:

> The jungle
> varies in the dream, but the dream does not:
> first, the loud and hideous conversations,
> then when they stop.

Something's still missing, though, something more specific. Eventually, it surfaces: I realize I've been thinking about what happens still further inside the dream, inside the jungle, about the iron cauldron in the middle of the deep, dark Africa of my imagination where the Hollywood white man, or his beautiful companion, gets boiled for dinner.

I choose in the end to generalize the language just enough to connect the feeling of being outnumbered to the New Year's party where there's a similarly hostile and hungry crowd with no dietary compunctions.

The jungle
varies in the dream, but the dream does not:
dragged to a clearing where the cannibals wait,
first the loud and hideous conversations,
then when they stop.

It isn't the end of the world, Marion's saying.
Janice disagrees. Look at sunspots, the pull
of impending disaster, where the idea of progress leads.
Marion isn't objective either.
She was thinking about her own personal situation.

Midnight, a second after
midnight, and what if it's not? It's a huge
responsibility and these are men,
if not smaller, then no huger than the average,
weak: they must entertain their doubts. What if
their white and beating hearts deceive them? What if time
and the marking of time aren't alike? Or worse.
In Zeno's paradox, where the arrow never quite arrives
at its target, anyone can be immortal, poised.

What does the poem mean, "Or worse"? The timekeeper's lost in a dream of fear that time isn't real, that it has no meaning, that we're lost and without bearings in an indifferent universe; conversely, that it's all too real and cannot be escaped; or finally, that both these unappealing prospects may be true at once. He rejects Zeno's solution as a witty, bitter mathematical joke. To the timekeeper's relief, when

He cries out, somebody
slaps him on the back, gives him a glass
of champagne, a young girl kisses him on the mouth
with her red lips: Happy New Year! like a welcome, a prayer
to the other side of the wilderness
in what's even more of a surprise, his native tongue.

The crisis passes. The timekeeper wakes from his jungle dream. The poem ends as time, or its illusion, safely and comprehensibly resumes.

There comes a point sometimes in the rewriting of a poem when it resembles the working out of a jigsaw puzzle. Some piece may be missing in the middle that prevents the poem from being finished because the ending depends on an unformed image or its wording. For some time, for example, I was unable to complete the poem "Doomed" because I couldn't get the middle lines to work. In the second stanza, two strangers are driving across the central plains on their way from the East Coast to the West:

> Your companion pops No-Doz, flips the radio dial
> every few minutes to make sure he is
> where he thinks he is

Then came a hole where his confusion enters, and below that the poem resumed with a piece that had survived from the original version:

> You swear you can smell the sea
> and he loves it, no question
> California, the two of you, the future

and there it sat. What needed to happen was for me to see, or hear, that the word "where" stands for the word "who," that landscape and identity are one, that the companion is afraid he'll get stuck, despite the illusion of movement, forever. The shift in that one word, the fitting of that piece, made the difference.

> Your companion pops No-Doz, flips the radio dial
> every few minutes to make sure he is
> where he thinks he is, no fool
> like the deejays spinning blind in their booths.
> Every station repeats the same news.
> You swear you can smell the sea
> and he loves it, no question

As soon as I had the image of the deejays, I could finish the puzzle with

> California, the two of you, the future
>
> you've heard a hundred times before, it's a hit
> and it shines on the other side of this landscape
> like the light from the setting sun or a star, traveling
> at the same speed you are.

Of course, if you're traveling at the speed of light, you appear to yourself to be standing still. The woman in the poem is under no illusion that her situation or position is going to change; I was very much like her at the time of writing. Poems can give us private information like that about ourselves, the same way dreams can.

They can give us universally private information too. When poems, all poems, make their private information available through publication or performance, they become like public dreams, dreams we share, secrets about the human condition we sometimes dare to admit or think about only in this special context. We need poems, as we need dreams, for our mental, emotional, and spiritual health. We suppress them, individually or collectively, at our peril.

MICHAEL BURNS

Michael Burns grew up in Arkansas and received his M.F.A. degree from the University of Arkansas in Fayetteville. His volumes of poetry include *When All Else Failed* (1983), *And As For Darkness* (1987), *The Secret Names* (1994), and most recently *It Will Be All Right in the Morning* (1998). A recipient of the Missouri Writers Biennial Award and a National Endowment for the Arts grant, Burns has edited essay collections about the work of Miller Williams and Mona Van Duyn. He is professor of English at Southwest Missouri State University in Springfield.

ON THE PAST, POETRY, AND DREAM

grew up in the farm country of the mid-South, and my life as a boy was one that carried forward the rituals of the ancestral hunter gatherers. With friends, or alone, I jumped the rabbits from the brush piles and cotton patches, and I waited at dawn or twilight for my prey to stir from their nests high in the trees. I watched my fishing line for movement that meant some other, secret thing that might be a flathead or blue channel cat had answered from the watery side of the world. Like the night creatures, the possum and raccoon, I knew the woods where wild mulberries grew, the fencerows of persimmon. I shared my hunting and fishing and foraging space with the cottonmouth and rattlesnake and water moccasin.

In that rural community, a poor, satellite tribe, we gathered three times a week with neighbors at the local church. It was built of wood and brick, without the adornment of stained glass or lofted ceilings; it was still our temple. I learned the songs and prayers of our god and heaven, not as if they were metaphors but as if they described a place and power as real as the rivers and fields of my own heart. Did we believe in magic? When I was nine, the preacher stood with me in that little room we kept filled with water, and he lowered me down into it, and—this is important—*all the way under it.* The evil, though invisible, that had colored and controlled my life was washed away. I came up clean.

Like most of the local children, I grew up picking and chopping cotton. The job brought, with its bone-fatigue, a small romance—the forced intimacy with strangers who shared the work, sometimes Mexicans; the wistfulness of lying on my back at the end of the day in a wagon filled with cotton, feeling the dew come on and watching the stars appear. I liked then and still like the smell of things—rain far away, freshly plowed fields, the ripening cotton.

We didn't know much history. For all we knew (and later discovered was pretty much the truth), the parents or grandparents of the present farmers had been the ones who settled the land. They had drained the sloughs and cut the trees and been the first to wrestle the earth into cultivation. That is, they were the first except for the Indians. I had only a vague notion of who these Indians could have been, but nothing in my life—not the rush of a kill, or the thrill of a catch—delighted me as much as the revelation of their presence in touch with my own flesh, when I knelt in the dirt to pick up an arrowhead. Their tangible past met a need in me that lay so deep it has become a subject for many of my poems and the primary treasure of my adult dreams.

Because thinking about the connection between my past, my poetry, and my dreams forces me to consider what memories and emotions I've buried, and how I unearth them, I have to admit to myself that I face an emptiness. I believe it is directly connected to the distance I've put between my present self and the life that I once lived. Or maybe it's not just a distance between myself and the past, but also between me and a necessary confrontation/relationship with the physical world. Some days I'm not sure whether poetry, especially my own poetry, is a part of the problem or the solution. As a writer and a teacher of writing, I inhabit a world made up of language, and how tangible can that ever be? More shadowy than dreams.

I love my dreams. I dream often, and I entertain, terrify, and mystify myself with my dreams. I encounter "stranger" women whose breasts secrete blue flame; I recognize the devil (whom I don't believe in, in waking life) as the giant in a batman costume who is swimming in my water-filled basement; I fly like—well, like a man flying—over the seats in huge auditoriums; and I unearth the secret stores of Indian artifacts where they have lain for centuries, in the common fields. But I seldom use any of these amazing, psychic moments as material for my poems. As stories, they don't hold together very well, and as "deep" images, they just seem too private or maybe even too generic in their implications.

Then maybe the most important and reliable connection between my poetry and my dreams is, finally, their shared purpose. At their most powerful source, they heal me. They affirm a place in my life that is shaped by the richness of my past. On a good day or night when I most need to fill the emptiness, I go off into their rivers and fields, hunting and gathering.

NICHOLAS CHRISTOPHER

© MARION ETTLINGER

Nicholas Christopher is the author of six books of poetry, most recently *In the Year of the Comet* (1992) and *5°* (1995), both published by Viking Penguin, and *The Creation of the Night Sky* (1998), published by Harcourt Brace. He is also the author of three novels, *The Soloist* (Viking, 1986), *Veronica* (Dial, 1996), and *A Trip to the Stars* (Dial, 1999). He has published a nonfiction book, *Somewhere in the Night: Film Noir and the American City* (Free Press, 1997), and has edited two poetry anthologies. Christopher has received awards from the Guggenheim Foundation, the Academy of American Poets, and the Poetry Society of America. He lives in New York City.

OUT OF THE UNDERWORLD
Poetry and Dreams

A poem emanating directly from a dream—actively apprehended by the poet—is akin to a snapshot of the psychic underworld. In fact, the poem may more resemble a sequence of snapshots (like those small flip-page books at the turn of the century depicting a trapeze artist or a dancing dog that simulated, and preceded, "moving pictures") or even a fragment of film. But in apprehending the dream we are already shaping and defining it. A camera lens may capture an image when its shutter is snapped, but the photograph that emerges later, dependent on the chemicals in the developing pan, the timing of procedures, the nuances of printing paper, and so on, often "looks like" something else altogether. How a poet may remember a vivid dream—and record its elements in, say, a journal or letter—and how he may reconfigure that dream aesthetically, thematically, and psychologically in order to produce a poem vivifying to others are two distinctly different propositions.

The psychologist James Hillman has written that "dream-work, like any work of *poesis* (the making of images in words), is shaped not only by its content but also by its manner of presentation." He goes so far as to say that "dreams come in styles; we might say, in literary genres." And without mentioning William Blake, Hillman echoes him. Blake lambasted the empiricism of Hume and Locke as the deathly opposite (a kind of spiritual nullification, in fact) to his own belief in the transformative primacy of the poetic imagination. Of the latter, Blake wrote, "One Power alone makes a Poet: Imagination, The Divine Vision"; and in *Jerusalem* (71:17), he makes his clearest statement on the subject: "In your own Bosom you bear your Heaven and Earth & all you behold; tho' it appears Without, it is Within, in your Imagination, of which this World of Mortality is but a Shadow." Compare this with Hillman, who wrote:

> We perceive images with the imagination, or, better said, we imagine them rather than perceive them. . . . The error of empiricism is its attempt to employ sense perception everywhere, for hallucinations, feelings, ideas, and dreams. Because the dream speaks in images, or even *is* images—which is what the Homeric *oneiros* meant—because dreaming is imaging, our instrument for undistorted listening can only be the imagination. Dreams . . . can be answered only by the imagination.

For the poet, this means answering a powerful psychic summons with the subtlety of his art, separating and distilling the essence of the dream—which he must view as an incident occurring in the psychic underworld—just as he would refine the components of an incident in this world after drawing them from his memory.

Heraclitus said that "sleepers are workers" (Fragment 75), doing their dream work. It may be that there are particularly industrious poets who can scan their dreams for poetic material in the first chill of morning, but I am not one of them. I have no doubt that a number of my poems—perhaps more than I think—have grown out of dreams which are now scrambled, camouflaged, or meshed within the framework of other, fresher dreams, or are forgotten altogether. I am aware, too, of every so often finding in my dreams images and symbols lifted from poems I have written. But with absolute clarity I can only remember four poems of mine—out of six published volumes and a healthy group of as-yet-unpublished and other never-to-be-published poems—that have proceeded directly from my dream life. Already I get queasy making such a statement, with its implicit distinction that my dream life and imaginative life are separate entities, when I know that at the very least they share the same, highly fluid frontier. That said, whether my poetic imagination is a tributary off the great river of my dream life, or whether they are parallel streams in the same sometimes fertile landscape, I can't say. Whether the process that has allowed me to compose these particular four poems is a phenomenon of cross-pollination or of a uroboros-like self-devouring circularity is not clear to me. Somehow I am convinced that the day I can draw such a conclusion empirically will be the day the link between these two currents in me will have dried up, been diverted, or been rendered moot by a chthonic epiphany I cannot possibly foresee at this time.

But perhaps the poems themselves, speaking for themselves, and a brief recounting of the circumstances under which they were composed, will shed more light on these questions than I possibly could, standing back from them with a cold eye. The first poem must speak for itself, because it is literally the retelling of a dream I had; I can think of no other poem of mine that so closely follows one of my recollected dreams. I wrote the poem several days after having the dream, the summer night I arrived at the westernmost Hawaiian island of Kaua'i after a fifteen-hour journey, on three different airplanes, from New York City. I usually sleep five to seven hours, but this particular night, exhausted and exhilarated, and after a midnight swim in the ocean, I slept deeply, without interruption, for ten hours. This poem, I should add, emerged very cleanly in early drafts and went through fewer revisions than the majority of my poems, as if much of the work on it had already been done in my head.

After a Long Illness

A man lighter than air enters
the glass house, switches on
every lamp, and turns the radio
to a station broadcasting
the sound of birds' wings flapping
skyward over a deep lake at dawn.

He pours himself a glass of water
from a tall pitcher on which
a crane, drinking from a pitcher,
has been etched in the enamel.
He makes a sandwich of brightly colored
pieces of paper and slices it in half.

Opening a window, he reels in
a clothesline with two billowing
sheets, white as ocean clouds,
and lays them on a bed so high
he would need a ladder to reach it
were he not lighter than air.

He reclines on the bed with a book
of photographs of birds in flight
and gazes up through the glass room
at the full moon and the stars.
In the morning, a quart of milk
is left at the door, a letter is

dropped through the mail slot,
the lawn is mowed and the shrubs
trimmed, but there is no one home.
A woman arrives in a see-through
raincoat, switches off the lamps
and the radio, climbs to the roof,

and lets out a kite on a long string.
Winding the string in hours later,
she finds it attached, not to the kite,
but to a man who is fast asleep,
trailing vapors, his arms folded
across his chest like wings.

In the second poem, "The Anonymous Letter," I appropriated,
and reconfigured, the elements of a very brief portion of a much longer
dream. At the time I dreamed it, in the dead of winter in New York, it
was the other parts of the dream—thinly disguised representations of an

utterly mundane, unpleasant problem (I was tangentially involved in a tortuous legal proceeding)—that distracted my waking mind. But months later I discovered that the splinter elements of the dream which came to comprise this poem had attached themselves to my imagination.

The Anonymous Letter

suggests it was in a previous life
I emerged from a long tunnel
echoing sharply with horses' hooves

and a cradle moon just a sliver
in a bracelet of stars
was poised above the steep cliff

from which a cloud of birds veered
pitch-black toward the breakers
a ship's light rising and falling over the horizon

and someone on a bluff calling to me
the wind drowning out the words
I hear now years later when I approach the sea

Another poem, "The Lights of Siena as Seen from Florence in a Dream," is a real curiosity to me because its inception lay in my dreaming of myself actually coming on the poem's title. This happened sometime in 1987, and it was fully six years before I wrote the poem itself, and another three before I completed it to my satisfaction. In that time, I published three books of poems, all of which, at one time or another, I thought the poem would make its way into. In fact, I finally published it in 1998, in my sixth book of poems. So, unlike "After a Long Illness," which was literally dreamt, composed, and then published immediately afterward in a magazine and in one of my books, "The Lights of Siena as Seen from Florence in a Dream" had a slow and tortuous history.

The dream struck me as strange even while it was happening—from within—which is I think why I uncharacteristically included the words "in a dream" in the title. The poem emerged so literally that I felt I had no choice. I dreamt myself sitting by a starlit window slowly turning the pages of a large, leatherbound book—thick, heavy pages—until in the middle of the book I came on a page with only a single line of text which slowly swam into focus: "The Lights of Siena as Seen from Florence in a Dream." The line was clearly positioned on the page as a title—a title without a poem. I woke up—it was a steamy midsummer night and the air conditioner in my bedroom was streaming waves of icy air over me—and on an index card scrawled the title. The next morning I found the card beside my alarm clock, read it, and found it had little effect on me before I filed it away. Nine years later, this is the poem (here after many revisions) that I wrote:

The Lights of Siena as Seen from Florence in a Dream

This is the door by which you will leave me forever.
As always, it stands ajar, admitting the cold
rays of stars that will help you navigate the darkness.

In an ink blot a woman in blue deciphered the future.
Not hers, or yours, but mine.
She wore earrings carved of bloodred stone:

hardened embers, highly polished, that sprayed
seaward from a volcano on the Tropic of Cancer
ten thousand years before her birth.

She offered me a glass of clear tea
and drew the curtains from a rain-streaked
window overlooking a broad expanse

in which the sun, minutes from setting,
was streaming flames over the horizon,
igniting the poplars like torches.

I walked all night along a road soft with dust.
The pack on my back was heavy as stone.
Faceless coins jangled in my pocket

and the hands on my watch were moving in opposite
      directions.
Like fingers, the wind ran through my hair.
Walking in step to my heartbeat, I crossed a vast plain

and took this hotel room in Florence where I saw
far to the south the lights of Siena, like the stars
that even then were leading you away from me.

The fourth poem also has a bizarre origin—this time rooted in far
more traceable ways to my waking life. And the lag time here between
the dream and the poem was seventeen years. In 1973, traveling around
Europe, I was staying in a hotel in Barcelona, having crossed the Pyrenees
from France the previous week in a small car. It was an inexpensive hotel,
but I had obtained a room with a wonderful balcony that overlooked a
small plaza ringed with old shade trees and centered by a beautiful circu-
lar fountain. At the fountain's center, cascaded by spray, was a marble
statue of a young woman with upturned eyes. Directly behind the fountain was a tall white church with a steeple in which melodious bells rang
at vespers. When I wasn't roaming the city, I spent many hours sitting on
that balcony, reading, drinking coffee or an aperitif, and napping. On one
such occasion, having dozed off, I was awakened suddenly by a cry and a
loud splash. It was dusk, but the streetlights had not yet been turned on,
so everything in the plaza below was indistinct to me at first. When I did
focus clearly, I saw no one; this was strange in itself, because there were
usually people milling in the plaza except at siesta on the hottest days.
Because of the fountain's placement below the church, I had several
times that week thought it reminded me of one of those dime-sized pools
into which daredevil divers plunge from great heights at carnivals. So at
that moment I became convinced that someone had dived off the church
steeple into the fountain, making the loud splash that woke me up. Of
course there was no evidence of this—for example, a body, dead or alive,
in the fountain itself. In the ensuing minutes, scanning the plaza, I could

discover no explanation for the splash, and assuring myself that I had imagined it, I put the entire episode aside and went out to dinner. I remained unsettled, drank some wine, and slept badly that night. If I had any dreams, I didn't remember them the next morning.

A couple of weeks later, I left Barcelona, driving up the Costa Brava, back over the Pyrenees into France. A girl I had met in Paris months before had flown down and joined me, so I had company now. Just before we left Barcelona, the newspapers were filled with the story of a once-famous acrobat who fell while attempting a dangerous stunt atop the enormous, unfinished Gaudí cathedral. In trying to resuscitate his career, he had come to a tragic end. But it was only when we reached France, and the incidents recounted in the poem below occurred, that I recalled the splash I had heard from my balcony in that waking dream (or was it?). I didn't include that part of the story in the poem; maybe the most fantastical element in a poem comprised of such elements, it simply didn't fit, overpowering all the rest. So here is a dream poem, written in 1990, in which the most interesting oneiric possibility—a piece of my own life in which dreams and so-called reality had so confusedly intermingled—had to be excluded to preserve the integrity of the poem's "dream" qualities:

Outside Perpignan in Heavy Rain

The trees sway darkly
along the black wall with its vines.
For shelter, a cat squeezes
between the steel bars over a window.
This is where the caretaker lives,
catty-corner to the cemetery,
with a door the color of stone.

We've just descended the mountains,
windshield wipers slapping mud
while we talked about the acrobat
who was in the papers yesterday:
how he attempted
to perch blindfolded on the highest
steeple of the Gaudí cathedral.

Through the gate, in the first
row of gravestones, a statue
depicts a young woman
raising her hand to her face:
Is she about to touch her forehead?
to tear out her hair?
to dig her nails into her cheek?
to stifle a cry
or make the sign of the cross?

In this life which is the only life
it is a gesture we see every day.
You say someone in a position
to know told you it's easy
to learn about these things
without learning anything at all.
Without ever running out of questions.
When that acrobat fell in bright sunlight,
did all the women in the street raise
their hands to shield their eyes?

My most recent poem is a long poem, novella-length, called
Night Journal. It consists of thirty-seven entries, written on different
nights over a nine-month period. The poem is broken up according to
the actual dates of its composition. I made the entries, each in its
entirety, on the dates which subdivide the poem, and I only began an
entry when I knew I would complete it that same night in one sitting—
exactly as I would keep a personal journal. At the same time, the action
of the poem occurs on a single timeless night, and the night journal, far

from being a conscious compendium of my own worldly activities, turned into a chronicle of those events which I set in motion in my imagination on the first day of the new year—the traditional starting point for a personal journal. In retrospect, this night journal became far more personal than any such traditional journal I might have kept over those same nine months, filled with characters out of my dreams and people in my life, mingling back and forth as if through a sieve. Some nights I was dealing with very raw material, poetically speaking, converting—or subverting—it immediately to the needs of my narrative.

In fact, while writing *Night Journal,* I wondered if the novelist in me, even more than the poet, had succumbed to the hopeless temptation of attempting to shape dream material into a coherent narrative while I was newly emergent from the dream, or worse, still inside it. Or perhaps the very hopelessness of such an effort produced a tension that enabled the poem to take shape as it did. Even if that is so, I believe that no matter how hard a poet may try to force the issue, it is his dream material, emerging in its own time and assuming its own form—and with its own very particular set of dynamics—that will truly shape his poems. Sometimes he is aware of this material's content; most often he is not. If the material is to become a vessel that both emblematizes and accommodates the dreams of others, the poet's imagination must be its furnace, firing, hardening, and preserving it, turning the ephemeral into something permanent, and permanently transformative.

SARAH COTTERILL

LAURA TANGUSSO

Sarah Cotterill grew up in rural New York. She received a B.A.
from Swarthmore College and an M.F.A. from the Iowa Writers'
Workshop, where she was a Teaching-Writing Fellow. She has
been a Yaddo Fellow and has received grants from the Maryland
Arts Council and the National Endowment for the Arts. Her
first book, *The Hive Burning*, was published by Sleeping Bird
Press, and her second, *In the Nocturnal Animal House*, by Purdue
University Press. Ms. Cotterill lives in Maryland with her husband, Philip, and three sons.

IMPRESSIONISM AND THE ARMY CORPS OF ENGINEERS

Sometimes the poem is a record of a half-remembered dream, an attempt to get it, accurately, down. Or, if not a record of the dream, then its completion.

In the early 1970s I read a brief, sketchy news account: a southern Ohio valley had been flooded—the work of an Army Corps of Engineers dam. The area, home to descendants of early settlers, had been thinly populated. The Army Corps evacuated everyone—voluntarily or un—leaving small ghost towns to be submerged. At least one pioneer graveyard was inundated. The landscape was transformed from hardscrabble hillside farms and quirky hamlets to a reservoir and "recreational lake," bland but serviceable for boaters and sport fishermen. In my mind's eye the countries of before and after became superimposed—the lives of the settlers going on uninterrupted in the valley, while tourists roared overhead in their Evinrudes, or retirees cast trawl lines into the new lake. Some of my own family had homesteaded southern Ohio in the 1840s. Distant kin still lived nearby. I wondered if their names figured among the displaced living or the anonymous dead of that drowned cemetery.

Another image surfaced, competed for voice when, some years later, I worked this material into a poem. In Mary Cassatt's "The Boating Party" we see, as in a snapshot, a woman in Victorian dress. A child of one or two in her lap, she sits in the bow of a boat, facing the man who rows them across a broad lake. His back is to the viewer; his head is at a slight angle, looking at the woman, or past her. But the woman's eyes are fixed on his face, as are the child's. The woman's expression is not quite readable—worry? resignation? entreaty? accusation? Whatever the sum of her emotion, her face doesn't much convey pleasure. One wonders whose idea this trip was. The woman's arm is locked around the child's waist, reflexively I think, as if the toddler would squirm and flop into the water at any moment, without her vigilance. Perhaps what has passed between the man and the woman, reflected in the intensity of her gaze, has nothing to do with the child: "You're leaving me?" or "You forgot the lunch?" We're strangers witnessing . . . something. The little drama we glimpse here lodged in memory as I encountered it daily—a museum print hanging above my desk. The voices of my own young children floated through the house as I wrote.

These, then, were the materials that dream went to work on. Where dream left off and the poem, "Coming of the Dam," began, I don't remember. Where detail of the dream was altered in the writing process, I have only the limited evidence of the poem itself. Here are the settlers contemplating the reservoir:

> It is the first rain on a new lake:
>
> on the outskirts of early towns
> drenched ancestors look up   through coloring oak and
>   sweet gum
> to where pass immigrant
> salmon   and a little higher   boats of
> the living with their lures . . .

Mary Cassatt's boaters turn up in the poem, though so changed as to be beyond recognition. The iIntimate trio of man-woman-child has become a flotilla. It's a fishing trip, for the men, at least. The women see to lunch and children, keeping a wary eye on men and weather. The dream/poem has this advantage over the painting: it can peer down into the water to check on its submerged towns, observe its ghosts:

When they lean out from the bow they never know
what could flare up from the water   snag:

It is that way with poems. You never know what could rise.

Coming of the Dam

I
It is the first rain on a new lake:

on the outskirts of early towns
drenched ancestors look up   through coloring oak and
      sweet gum
to where pass immigrant
salmon   and a little higher   boats of
the living with their lures—
crawlers, suet—

in mackinaws crossing to what they hope
is a better place   to catch their limit;

but sick of motion and squalling
the women not sure   anything like this
ought to be tried.

2
When they lean out from the bow they never know
what could flare up from the water<2>snag:
tree crown   steeple   resinous
plume
of cabin—lowlanders
who wanted a similar valley.
            A presence

pulls on the line:
          dawn   a woman
trying to be quiet with the
pans   letting them sleep,
her stove (radiant   untouchable)   taking the chill off
   mornings.

A woman who coiled her hair in the muggy summer   an old
    way,
someone who noticed the dampness
so bad in her hands   gripping

a valley with a reputation
for loam   fever   good brides,
with a calm that bordered on
river.

Men always checking the sky.

3

The sky's mackerel,
                    the men won't be hurried
from the curved tine of the hook   though the lake's filling
and lake weather not to be trusted.

The women   they can't believe it   waiting   the dusk so
sullen   absorbent   courting
a bad going back;

time to collect everything   sweetbreads and young feuding
in their accents   their cast-offs.

they've thought of the baskets,
the blankets   ready to
believe a long passage.

Setting off from the old flume of
the river   the old landing   it heads

inland by stages—fluent in lake but
taking its dialect back into hills.

Giving away the heavy bed as it leaves
but keeping an unmanageable
family   an heirloom of birds

a profile

a habit of waking

first and looking out over the bare water.

RACHEL HADAS

PHOTO BY DALE GRANT

Rachel Hadas is the author of ten volumes of poetry and prose. Her recent collection, *The Empty Bed* (1995), contains elegies for her mother as well as for friends who have died of AIDS. Hadas's poetry workshop at the Gay Men's Health Crisis in New York led to an influential anthology, *Unending Dialogue: Voices from an AIDS Poetry Workshop* (1991). Among her other volumes of poetry: *Pass It On* (1989) and *Mirrors of Astonishment* (1992). Her collection of selected poems, called *Halfway Down the*

Hall, is published by Wesleyan University Press (1998). A professor of English at Rutgers University, Hadas lives on New York's Upper West Side with her husband, the composer George Edwards, and their son, Jonathan.

POEMS AND DREAMS

reams and poems are engaged in some of the same tasks and use some of the same tools. Both, in my experience, somehow know and can convey unappealing truths to which the waking person, the person living her daily life in prose, seems to lack access. Or is it just courage that she lacks? I was writing poems foreshadowing the end of my first marriage long before I'd admitted to myself that it was ending. A dream informed me of my mother's fatal cancer a week or two before her diagnosis.

Both poetry and dreams often make lavish use of images; both often move laterally, erratically, by means of what I think of as lyric leaps. Both can be screamingly clear or hermetically difficult to construe. Both are mysterious in their provenance, seeming to come from deep within the self yet also reaching us as if from outside. Both can be zanily solipsistic, yet can also command an impersonal kind of authority.

It's not surprising, then, that for me, as for many poets, dreams are not only rich sources of imagery but something more. They feel like messages from another world, an intangible place that is nevertheless every bit as vivid and valid as the everyday world of waking reality.

As we all know, dreams often melt away, leaving, as Prospero put it, not a wrack behind. The medium I use for simultaneously fixing dreams in my memory and trying to make sense of them is poetry. It's hardly surprising, then, that many of the dreams I succeed in recalling touch upon the same themes many of my poems do. One such theme is people I loved, have lost, and continue to love. Three such poems follow, with a little commentary. One is about my friend Charles Barber; it was inspired by a dream several years after his death. The other two, about James Merrill, grew out of dreams within months of Merrill's death.

"Around Lake Erie and Across the Hudson" recalls and examines one of those dreams that seem to happen just before one wakes up and begins the day. This day was a day I went to work, commuting as usual from Manhattan to my teaching job at Rutgers in Newark, riding west across the Hudson as the sun rose. It seemed important to get the real journey across the river, as well as the dream journey around Lake Erie, into the poem.

The dawn dream had a vividness, clarity, and above all a joy I wanted to capture. The spare format of quatrains helped me pare away irrelevancies and highlight details such as the haircut, the sweater, and the precise seating arrangements in the car, even if I wasn't sure what these details meant.

I did know why Lake Erie was in my dream. The "you" of this poem, Charlie Barber, is a beloved friend who had died some years previously, but who in this remarkably happy and hopeful dream returns. (Even as I dreamed it, I understood that such a return was an impossibility, and that understanding too goes into the poem.) Charlie came from Cleveland, where his parents and sister still live. I've kept in touch with his family; but I've never been closer to Cleveland than the airport. Certainly I've never driven around Lake Erie, and I somehow doubt that the lake is as huge, sparkling, and blue as the white-capped, ocean-like expanse in my dream.

Why do we dream of our dear dead as and when we do? More than four years after Charlie's death, my grieving for him had lost its rawness. Was this dream a reminder of what I'd lost, or a reassurance as to how much I'd kept by way of memory and sheer feeling? Coming at the start of a long day, it did indeed make me want to give thanks as I rode west into New Jersey and the sun rose behind me: thanks for morning light, for consciousness, for life itself, of which mourning our dead is a part. Crossing the river came, as I worked on the poem, to seem less like a "true" detail than like part of the dream itself. Wasn't the Hudson really a version of the mythological river that separates sleep from waking, or the dead from the living? Both dreams and poems lend themselves to such deeper meanings, for both are worlds unto themselves, with their own mysterious laws.

Around Lake Erie and Across the Hudson

A rotten week, affections
grating against the grain.
I wake up, eyes beclouded
by the gift of a dream.

First an anxious journey,
directions barely heard,
lockers, crowds, and tunnels,
the destination blurred . . .

But then, ah! Calm perspective.
As if I were awake,
we three are slowly driving

You at the wheel, your sister
in front along with me.
Blue water, little whitecaps.
Brilliant October day.

You have a brand new haircut.
Your sweater's white and red.
Such vivid preparations—
as if life lay ahead.

Deliberately driving,
you cannot turn to me.
But conversation ripples
among us easily,

sister, friend, and brother
catching up: what's new?
And underneath the chitchat lie
two things we three know.

One, that we are joyful,
and two, this isn't real
miraculously coexist:
a miracle that still

tinges both past and future
with possibility,
although this outing never was
and will not ever be.

The shining lake: our chatter—
I carry them to work.
On New Jersey Transit
west out of New York

the rising sun behind the train
gilds pylons, bridge, gas tanks.
A purple cloud. A single gull.
I find I'm giving thanks.

I've dreamed about James Merrill many times, both during the twenty-six years of our friendship and since his death. In the two poems that follow, Merrill's death makes itself felt obliquely. These poems aren't joyful if fantastical reunions, like "Around the Lake and Across the River." Rather, they both in different ways explore the way a person no longer living is nevertheless central—a presence, a motivation.

In "May," Merrill is present, but just barely; he hurries away as if for an important appointment the nature of which is all too easy to imagine. In "Tea and a Dream," he is absent—"gone"—but in a sense all the more present. Both dreams contain large public structures—a lobby, an elevator—and are populated by groups of people—specifically, in "Tea and a Dream," by poets. This sense of a group is absolutely true to the feeling after Merrill's death of a circle of grieving friends, many of whom were poets. No one person could claim to have been central to Jimmy's life, but then no one had to bear the loss alone either. As Richard Kenney wrote to me at the time, "We all collapse a little; may it be toward each other."

And toward Merrill too. For both these poems, like "Around the Lake," use the second person, lyric poetry's distinctive way of turning toward the person to whom the poet speaks. The intimacy of apostrophe is in no way invalidated by the death of the person addressed.

Elizabeth Bishop dreamed at least once about George Herbert. Robert Frost did appear to me in a dream years ago—was it because as a child I'd met the famous old man? I don't dream, or haven't yet, of Sappho or Keats, Dickinson or Whitman. But I feel very fortunate that the poet who was my dear friend continues to be a living presence in my dreams.

May

The latest dream: a lofty hotel lobby,
honeycombed with entrances and exits.
Feeling weak, I find a corner, lean
against the pale gold alabaster wall,
and feel its coolness seep into my shoulders.
Suddenly you appear and hurry past me
on your way out. An open door, a car
waiting . . . I summon all my strength to say
before you vanish just how much I loved you.
I think you hear. You smile and then are gone.
The lobby like a hive, the steady stream
of transients moving in, out, up, and down;
empty and crowded world. Again alone,
I lean against the coolness of the stone.

Tea and a Dream

One eye open, on its little island
in the hotel moat, a green lagoon,
an alligator loiters. Four o'clock:
tea in the lobby with my hungry son.
Darjeeling, scones, meringues; but you are gone.
Pennies tossed into the fountain splash.
What do we wish for? Hush.

It is too late for thanks.
Repayment, rather—in what mortal coin?
You blow toward us in the soft Gulf breeze,
you shine on us in fitful springtime sun,
dismembered into myriad legacies,
scattered among the elements. You're gone,
an absence palpitating in my dream.

A black glass elevator,
sliding down the outside of a building,
shudders to a halt on the ground floor.
The passengers, all poets, getting out,
look at one another. It is dawn.
Has there been a party? You are gone.
Through avenues still silent we move off

in different directions
toward separate obligations
that await us—families, jobs, and time,
a lifetime's sum of days
on this strange foundation. You are gone.
The black box, emptied of its cargo, light,
rides again to a Parnassian height.

ANTHONY HECHT

Born in 1923, Anthony Hecht grew up in New York City and came of age just in time to experience the ferocity of World War II. His work counterpoints a dark vision of human folly with a great formal virtuosity. Among his books: *A Summoning of Stones* in 1954, *The Hard Hours* (winner of the 1968 Pulitzer Prize), *Millions of Strange Shadows* (1977), *The Venetian Vespers* (1979), *The Transparent Man* (1990), *Collected Earlier Poems* (1990), and *Flight Among the Tombs* (1994). Recently, he published two books of criticism, *The Hidden Law: The Poetry of W. H. Auden* (1993) and *On the Laws of the Poetic Art* (1995). Winner of the Bollingen

Prize and the Prix de Rome, Hecht has also served as poetry consultant to the Library of Congress. He taught at Bard College, then at the University of Rochester. He presently lives in Washington, D.C., where he is University Professor of Literature, Emeritus, at Georgetown University.

MISSING THE BOAT

our topic prompted thoughts about how many poets (and not a few writers of fiction) have called upon the dreamworld for their sources. As Jocasta says in *Oedipus Rex*, meaning to be reassuring to her second husband, "All men dream that they marry their mothers." I started out to make a hasty list of poets to whom the dreamworld was important, and found immediately these names: Langland, Auden, Bishop, Merrill, Shelley, Swinburne, Tennyson, Coleridge, Eliot, Dylan Thomas, Cavafy, Rilke, Rimbaud, Baudelaire, Yeats, Robert Penn Warren, Mark Strand, John Donne . . . at which point I stopped to wonder if there were any poets who did *not* rely on this fertile source.

For myself, I can say that, like many others, I have had recurrent dreams betokening anxiety, and usually taking the shape and scenario of finding myself rushing to a depot, a station, or a dock in the hope of getting aboard some vehicle or vessel, and at the final moment, failing. This was a frequent dream when I was young, and often enough in the dream I missed school tests or exams. There was no consolation in the thought that perhaps missing the test was better than flunking it. I was always brought awake in a cold sweat. A good deal later in my life, during what was surely a protracted interval of profound unhappiness, in which my first marriage was disintegrating, this early dream pattern combined itself with an image out of a painting by Watteau. The painting, *The Departure for Cythera*, is a lively, seeming joyous representation of crowds of richly fashionable and elegantly clad women, escorted by dapper and cultivated men, all preparing to embark for the island sacred to the goddess of love. Playing about the sails, the shroud-lines and the mast are bevies of tiny cupids, playful and buoyant. One art historian has commented regarding this painting:

> ancient mythology and eighteenth-century custom combine to form a world that appeared entirely real to Watteau's contemporaries. They themselves become dream figures and in Watteau's paintings they were able to enter into the lofty regions of the supernatural world previously denied to them. . . . But would not this illusion be followed by profound melancholy? There is a hint of melancholy in all Watteau's paintings; it is one of the characteristic features of his style."[1]

In my poem, which is titled "Clair de Lune," the ship departs for those sacred regions of unblemished love, leaving behind two persons, a man and a woman, abandoned at some vast emptied estate, and isolated from one another. To be sure, the Watteau and my elaboration upon it serve to disguise strong personal feeling from direct sight of the reader. But this is what dreams always do. They present us with their truths in elaborate, sometimes indecipherable disguise.

Clair de Lune

Powder and scent and silence. The young dwarf
Shoulders his lute. The moon is Levantine.
It settles its pearl in every glass of wine.
Harlequin is already at the wharf.

1. Michael Schwarz, *The Age of the Rococo* (London: Pall Mall Press, 1971), pp. 14–15.

The gallant is masked. A pressure of his thumb
Communicates cutaneous interest.
On the smooth upward swelling of a breast
A small black heart is fixed with spirit gum.

The thieving moment is now. Deftly, Pierrot
Exits, bearing a tray of fruits and coins.
A monkey, chained by his tiny loins,
Is taken aboard. They let their moorings go.

Silence. Even the god shall soon be gone.
Shadows, in their cool, tidal enterprise,
Have eaten away his muscular stone thighs.
Moonlight edges across the empty lawn.

Taffeta whispers. Someone is staring through
The white ribs of the pergola. She stares
At a small garnet pulse that disappears
Steadily seaward. Ah, my dear, it is you.

But you are not alone. A gardener goes
Through the bone light about the dark estate.
He bows, and, cheerfully inebriate,
Admires the lunar ashes of a rose,

And sings to his imaginary loves.
Wait. You can hear him. The familiar notes
Drift toward the old moss-bottomed fishing boats:
"Happy the heart that thinks of no removes."[2]

This is your nightmare. Those cold hands are yours.
The pain in the drunken singing is your pain.
Morning will taste of bitterness again.
The heart turns to stone, but it endures.

Dream poems about the touchy subject of personal pain not only
legitimately employ the characteristic evasions that belong to dreams,

---

2. This is the last line of a song, set by John Dowland, which I have long cherished, and
which begins, "Fine knacks for ladies, cheap, choice, brave, and new."

but take advantage as well of literary indirections. The powder and scent of the first line are feminine adornments, but also eighteenth-century details that go with peruques. The silence belongs equally to the soundless and motionless painting by Watteau, and to the absence of communication between the two people left behind and the real people behind the poem. The setting of the moon-pearl in the glass of wine is meant to recall the amorous extravagance of Cleopatra, as described in Pliny, and referred to in the final act of Jonson's *Volpone*. The commedia dell'arte, another favorite subject of Watteau, colors the opening stanzas, and is meant to lend a certain zest and excitement to the proceedings, as well as an erotic flavor. The monkey, for instance, was symbolic of incontinent lust, and is used for such symbolic purposes in *The Merchant of Venice*, when Shylock learns that the money Jessica has stolen from him was in part used to purchase a pet monkey. With the departure of the ship, images of decay and death set in: the shadows "eating away" at the statue, the "white ribs" of the pergola, the "pulse" that disappears, and "ashes of a rose." The "moss-bottomed fishing boats" contrast unfavorably with the elegant vessel that bears away all the lovers to Cythera; in addition, one can tell it's "moss-bottomed" because it is upside-down, that is, disused. The Dowland line is rich in irony as used here. In its original context it meant that those people were fortunate who were content with their life and love. But the lucky people in this poem are those who have indeed removed to the island of Venus. The gardener inhabits an ashen garden, and sings because he is drunk. The stone in the last line is the same stone as the carven god who, encroached upon by the eating shadows, will soon be gone.

It may be that this commentary sounds like outright "contrivance." But it must immediately be declared that dreams themselves, though apparently "effortless" as we dream them, are genuine contrivances, cunning evasions, as well as cryptic declarations of truths that are urgent and important. Doubtless it is next to impossible to unpack the full burden of most important dreams. Doubtless, also, our attempts to recall and reconstruct our dreams are themselves imperfect and corrupted by motives, fears and longings of which we are unaware or ashamed or otherwise eager to suppress. Literary dreams are often as eloquent as so-called "real" dreams, and I vividly remember dreams by a number of characters in *Crime and Punishment*. If these were no more than Dostoyevsky's fictive genius they nevertheless carry the perfect authority and credibility of genuine dreams. In this poem, in any case, my aim was not to convey to a reader the quality and degree of personal pain I was feeling; it was to create a scene and situation of symbolic sadness, even of anguish, but costumed and decorated in a carefully stylized way that, perhaps both for reader and author, served to mute whatever is personal in the poem.

EDWARD HIRSCH

A confirmed insomniac, Edward Hirsch titled his first collection *For the Sleepwalkers* (1981). The book received much recognition, including the Lavan Younger Poets Award from the Academy of American Poets. His second volume, *Wild Gratitude* (1986), received the National Book Critics Circle Award. Since then he has published *The Night Parade* (1989), *Earthly Measures* (1994), and *On Love* (1998). Hirsch was given a MacArthur Foundation grant in 1998. He teaches at the University of Houston.

SLEEPLESSNESS

know almost nothing about sleep. I have sampled its mysteries, I have tasted its (forbidden) pleasures, but its fullness evades me, its rich soothing body. I know even less about dreams. Everyone has a share of the dream kingdom, a stake in the dreamworld, but mine is a minor one. There are writers who build huge gothic mansions in the rolling countryside of sleep, but I merely lease a room in someone else's apartment building crouched by the side of a busy road. All night trucks lumber by and the ground rumbles underfoot. I own nothing here.

Poets are reputed to be great somnambulists. I am not. I love daydreams and dusky reveries, the nocturnal outings of consciousness, the infinite starry spaces of the night mind, but full-fledged dreams escape me. I, too, must have a nightly supply of dreams—everyone does—but mine seem to vanish into thin air as soon as I feel the first vague stirrings of consciousness in the early morning. They are ghosts fading in the blue tint of dawn, they are dark shadows fleeing into the walls. I turn left and right, I look back and every dream becomes Eurydice disappearing into the fog of the netherworld. She is the irretrievable beloved.

I suppose my natural habitat is insomnia—I know every foot of its rugged terrain—and yet I, too, have felt the delicious thrill of collapsing into sleep. There are long nights in my writing life when I suddenly come up against a blank wall. I simply cannot formulate the next line, the next sentence. I have lost the path, the trail has gone cold, continuity evades me. In desperation I pass out—pass over—into unconsciousness, and all night I feel an odd stuttering in the brain, the rhythm of words repeating themselves over and over again in the back of my mind, like a mantra. This doesn't feel like dreaming so much as a kind of obscure underground thinking, a graphology of the night mind. I wake up with a start and as soon as I sit down at my desk I feel a fresh line, a fresh thought, being delivered up to me, like a postal service from the deep. I remember nothing. And yet the letters have sifted through unconsciousness, and my restless ungrammatical sleep has given me back a poetic fluency . . .

I have been a nonsleeper for as long as I can remember. Wakefulness is mother's milk to me. Insomnia feels like something I inherited from my mother, like the shape of my nose or the color of my eyes. Give me a cup of spearmint tea and it comes back to me with a kind of Proustian recall: my mother's bare footsteps in the sleeping house, the sound of her moving lightly across the carpet in the drowsing hallway, her weight on the stairs. Soon I am following her down to the first floor of our house. It feels like the ground floor of being.

As a child I had terrible asthma attacks—I can still work up a healthy bout of nonbreathing—and I vividly recall those long nights with my mother in the kitchen of our two-story house. Somewhere I am seven years old again and she is talking me back, talking me down, from the crazed tower of my wheezing. I am listening to her soothing voice and breathing in the minty steam, I am giving up my panic, calming down, recovering my equilibrium, regaining the natural unthinking rhythm of breathing. I taste the leafy hot tea, and suddenly I can hear our low conspiratorial whispers going on late into the night, into the blue morning . . .

As a child I was also a sleepwalker. Sometimes I'd follow my mother down the stairs and it would take her a few moments to realize I was still unconscious, still sleeping. She'd find me opening the front door in the middle of a February night—where was I going in such a hurry?—or mumbling to myself in the middle of the living room. Once I pulled a huge bookshelf down onto my head because I was trying to climb up onto a moving train. Occasionally I'd wake up in the morning on the floor of my bedroom closet (how did I get there?), *and* sometimes I'd find my way back to bed on my own. Where do we go when we sleep? Where are we rushing with such urgency? And how do we wake up again and remain just one person when so many others shuffle through our restless minds at night? Hence the title poem of my first book in which I turned sleepwalking into a mysterious, metaphysical act of trust:

For the Sleepwalkers

Tonight I want to say something wonderful
for the sleepwalkers who have so much faith
in their legs, so much faith in the invisible

arrow carved into the carpet, the worn path
that leads to the stairs instead of the window,
the gaping doorway instead of the seamless mirror.

I love the way that sleepwalkers are willing
to step out of their bodies into the night,
to raise their arms and welcome the darkness,

palming the blank spaces, touching everything.
Always they return home safely, like blind men
who know it is morning by feeling shadows.

And always they wake up as themselves again.
That's why I want to say something astonishing
like: *Our hearts are leaving our bodies.*

Our hearts are thirsty black handkerchiefs
flying through the trees at night, soaking up
the darkest beams of moonlight, the music

of owls, the motion of wind-torn branches.
And now our hearts are thirsty black fists
flying back to the glove of our chests.

We have to learn to trust our hearts like that.
We have to learn the desperate faith of sleepwalkers who rise out of their calm beds

and walk through the skin of another life.
We have to drink the stupefying cup of darkness
and wake up to ourselves, nourished and surprised.

The poetic insomniac: one who takes the romantic connection between sleep and death a little too seriously. Panic ensues. It still seems to me astonishing that people drop off to sleep as if it were the most natural thing to do in the world. And they actually wake up again, refreshed. I wrote my first poem about insomnia in my late twenties, and I immediately recognized how much I like the situation that insomnia creates inside a poem. I like the dramatic sense—the solitary feeling—of a speaker who operates as a sole waking consciousness while darkness reigns and everyone else seems asleep. I like the feeling of vulnerability and tenderness. One of my first models was Gerard Manley Hopkins's late sonnet "I wake and feel the fell of dark, not day." Another was the poem "A Small Elegy" by the Czech poet Jiří Orten, which begins:

> My friends have left. Far away, my darling is asleep.
> Outside, it's as dark as pitch.
> I'm saying words to myself, words that are white
> in the lamplight . . .

Insomnia is the most solitary of experiences. I have done most of my deep reading late into the night, and thus books have paid me back for my sleeplessness with the richest of consolations. I have spent whole nights on fire with poetry. But there are other nights—panicky, exhausted—when sleep refuses to offer its solace, and consciousness feels like a torment. One falls into the black hole of four A.M.:

> The hour of nausea at middle age,
> the hour with its face in its hands,

the hour when no one wants to be awake,
the scorned hour, the very pit

of all the other hours,
the very dirge.

Five o'clock comes as "a life buoy in bruised waters. / The first broken plank of morning."

I have sometimes thought of insomniacs as an unacknowledged community. Anyone can join. Some come for only one night, some enter as chronic cases, some spend their entire nocturnal lives as members of our manic underground group. We recognize each other by secret looks, by the black bags under our eyes, by the first nervous signs of laughter. I feel great tenderness toward this quirky band of solitaries who never come together. It has seemed to me a little comical and desolate to think of calling for human help for so many of us. Hence the poem "I Need Help," which commences:

> For all the insomniacs in the world
> I want to build a new kind of machine
> For flying out of the body at night.
> This will win peace prizes, I know it,
> But I can't do it myself; I'm exhausted,
> I need help from the inventors.

The poem goes on to call for help from many people who obviously can't help—from weight lifters, from gardeners, from judges. It closes by literalizing the connection between sleep and death. I think of it as a kind of prayer for release from tormenting consciousness, for easeful sleep:

> And because I can't lift the enormous weight
> Of this enormous night from my shoulders
> I need help from the six pallbearers of sleep
> Who rise out of the slow, vacant shadows
> To hoist the body into an empty coffin.
> I need their help to fly out of myself.

Edward Hirsch

I think of writing poetry as my purchase on the night kingdom, a type of watchful reverie, a form of human making, an offering to the spiritual life, a kind of payment to eternity for the lifelong gift of sleep-lessness.

JOHN HOLLANDER

NATALIE CHARKOW

John Hollander's career as a poet started bright and
grew brighter. His first book, A *Crackling of Thorns*,
won the Yale Younger Poets Award in 1958. He followed this with some fifteen other volumes of
poetry, including *Movie Going and Other Poems*
(1962), *Reflections on Espionage* (1976), *In Time and
Place* (1986), *Selected Poems*, and *Tesserae* (both
1993). Hollander has also written five books of criticism, including *The Figure of Echo* (1981), *Melodious Guile* (1988), *The Gazer's Spirit* (1995), as well
as the influential handbook *Rhyme's Reason*. He was
awarded the Bollingen Prize and was a MacArthur
Fellow from 1990 to 1995. He is Sterling Professor
of English at Yale.

THE DREAM OF THE TRUMPETER

At the mountainous border of our two countries there is a village; it stands just below a pass, but some of the older houses lie higher up along the road, overlooking more of the valley than one might think. The border has never been heavily guarded, and our countries are peaceful. Theirs lies beyond the pass; in the other valley a large village looks up toward the mountains and toward us. The border itself is marked only by an occasional sign; but then there is the Trumpeter. His clear, triadic melodies break out through the frosty air, or through the swirling mists. From below, from above, the sound is commandingly clear, and it seems to divide the air as the border divides the land. It can be heard at no fixed intervals, and yet with a regularity which we accept, but cannot calculate. No one knows whether the Trumpeter is theirs or ours.

Epigraph to "The Head of the Bed"

This is a text. The dream which it embodies (or: surrounds? misremembers? embroiders upon with the kind of fierce fancy-work that becomes the fabric itself? interprets? reports?—even to fix on a verb here would be to enmesh a whole poetic theory), the dream related to it, is now barely accessible to me, the text having replaced it. I now cannot help but feel that it was originally dreamed *for* its textual role; although that feeling is itself a fiction which replaces buried, but probably useless, psychic history, it was a feeling that dawned on the occasion of incorporating the text in an earlier poem called "The Head of the Bed."

The dream as I remember it was a broad prospect—out at which I looked—all in the grays of etching and aquatint, of the mountain scene; I heard the trumpet, and knew in the dream that there was a Trumpeter, just as I had the sense (not from that kind of inner fiat, of axiom or identification revealed to the dreamer but from the landscape itself) that this was border territory. This was the kind of dream that arises in the fringes

65

of sleep, and I awoke at the sounds of the trumpeting—*at* rather than *to* them, as to an alarm clock or some other noise in the eternally awakened world which the trumpet call absorbed and transformed. It was as I awoke—just after it—that the question came to me in the light of my bedroom, and with a sense not of immediate urgency but of profound importance: *Was that trumpeter theirs or ours?*

It was some days later that I transcribed the dream in the present form, and I think that without knowing it I had even then my own recently completed (and, even to myself, still puzzling) "The Head of the Bed" in mind. This poem in fifteen parts is itself a figurative dream-journey, moving in and out of a protagonist's sleeping and waking states. Its first three parts, written early in 1971, all concern the shores of sleep as a place for the generation of images. The whole poem starts out:

> Heard through lids slammed down over darkened glass,
> Trees shift in their tattered sheets, tossing in
> Shallow sleep underneath the snoring wind.
>
> A dream of forests far inside such sleep
> As wakeful birds perched high in a dread wood,
> Brooding over torn leaves, might mutter of
> Rises over the pain of a snapped twig . . .

But although some of the episodes are explicitly dreamt in the poem's fictional narrative and some are actually encountered by the protagonist, there is only one scrap of material from any actual dream of my own (the flood scene, in section 12) anywhere in the poem. As I transcribed the Trumpeter dream—and perhaps even *by* transcribing it—I may have been completing, as well as glossing, the whole poem, which had been otherwise finished for the best part of a year.

When I added the text as an epigraph to "The Head of the Bed," I had already decided that the two countries in it were the realms of sleep and waking, and that the Trumpeter was a sort of liminal figure, a shore-warden who patrolled and celebrated whatever was at the line of division.

Attaching it to the poem entailed interpreting the last line, and thereby the whole text (the last line itself being an avowal of the unanswerability of the question into which I awoke from the dream). This was some years before I had read the ingenious theory of a young friend (now the distinguished medievalist Nicholas Howe), to the effect that, in Chaucer's *Reeve's Tale*, the place where the two Cambridge students avail themselves of the bodies of the miller's wife and daughter is made to be the village of Trumpington not merely because that village is in fact "nat fer fro Cantebrigge" but to pun on the French *tromper*, or deceiving. Perhaps my Trumpeter anticipated that conceit: a rubbing of the memorial brass of Sir Roger de Trumpington with a trumpet as his armorial bearing hung near my desk, and I had always brooded on the epithet of the fabled apocalyptic bugle, the Last Trump, both as a final card, kept in reserve, that won all for one and lost it for all the rest, as well as a *tromperie dernière*, a cruel eschatological joke. But if there was any *tromperie* in the trumpeting, it was, I realize now that I then concluded, elided into the higher cozenings of trope.

I should say something here about my earlier comment about not understanding my own poem "The Head of the Bed," at the time I added the prose epigraph. It seems superficially perverse or inaccurate to say that one has not understood something that he has written, revised, considered and so forth. In this case, I mean that although I was sure of every word in the text, sure of phrases and cadences, and certain of the order of the fifteen sections (which was, with some exceptions, not the mere order of composition, but rather a complex reconsidered response to that order), I could not at that point have written a plausible or coherent "argument" for the poem, or an essay on it. Indeed, I had the astonishing and invigorating experience of discovering, after it was published in full form in 1974 with an interpretive essay by Harold Bloom, that I had misconstrued the poem myself. Bloom had suggested that a female figure I had felt to be warm, reassuring and beneficent, who appears in the final section, was "not wholly distinguishable" from the final appearance of the other female figure, the witch Lilith, the patroness of bad nights, who shows up throughout the poem. I was, indeed, somewhat miffed at being incorporated into an interpretive figure, a figure designed to give symmetry and structure to a reading, rather than to cope, at just that point, with the text itself. I turned out to be quite wrong, and subsequent events in my life convinced me that the poem was indeed associating the two presences; that, like a dream, it knew more than I did about the harmful character of a force I had only felt to be protective heretofore.

Ironically, this later interpretive revision does not concern any actual "dream material" in the poem. Adding the epigraph was itself, I have said, an act of interpretation, of both the dream text and the poem; and the one phrase that manifestly connects the poem and the epigraph itself appears in the second tercet of the final section and, I now realize, significantly introduces the ambiguous beneficent figure who had entered the poem as I wrote it only in guise. The section opens with allusively apocalyptic images and leads up to the introduction of the warm companion whom I believed I was contrasting to the witch, "lilting Miss Noctae," later on in the episode:

> The bright moon offends him: he plucks it out;
> He opens all the seals of touch: he hears
> The whirlwinds of his breathing; then it comes:
>
> A last waking to a trumpet of light
> From warm lamps turns him over gravely toward
> Her long, bare figure, Lady Evening . . .

But it has only been the consideration, at the suggestion of the editor of this issue, of the Trumpeter dream that has led me to notice some of these patterns and juxtapositions, and some of the ways in which poem and dream seem to interpret each other. I have also been led to remember the first occasion on which I ever consciously referred to a dream of my own in any poem. For years I had never done so; the first poem to include anything from a dream was, I now remember, the first poem I ever wrote which left me with the feeling I have had much more frequently in recent years, of not knowing what my poem was really "about." The dream in question was a nightmare of early childhood, involving my maternal grandmother, to whom I was quite close, confronting me in a normal manner, but with her face totally crimson in color. The poem, written in 1965, involved actual recollections, too, of childhood fascination and terror at the sight of myself in a bedroom mirror in my darkened bedroom at night. In its final form "The Night Mirror" has its child protagonist, its frightened awakener, choose the terrors of dream over those of potential vision:

The Night Mirror

What it showed was always the same—
A vertical panel with him in it,
Being a horrible bit of movement
At the edge of knowledge, overhanging
The canyons of nightmare. And when the last
Glimpse was enough—his grandmother,
Say, with a blood-red face, rising
From her Windsor chair in the warm lamplight
To tell him something—he would scramble up,
Waiting to hear himself shrieking, and gain
The ledge of the world, his bed, lit by
The pale rectangle of window, eclipsed
By a dark shape, but a shape that moved
And saw and knew and mistook its reflection
In the tall panel on the closet door
For itself. The silver corona of moonlight
That gloried his glimpsed head was enough
To send him back into silences (choosing
Fear in those chasms below), to reject
Freedom of wakeful seeing, believing
And feeling, for peace and the bondage of horrors
Welling up only from deep within

> That dark planet head, spinning beyond
> The rim of the night mirror's range, huge
> And cold, on the pillow's dark side.

Syntactically, this poem is far from easy, and the narrative structure bore too much weight for me to do any more than accept it. While aware of all the grammatical ambiguities of the title phrase, "the night mirror"—that which mirrored *at* night, mirrored night itself, and so forth—and intentionally engaging them in the poem, I knew no more of the whole than that it had to be the way it was and, more mysteriously, that it was a very important poem for me even though, I must confess, I did not particularly like it. It was problematic in length, in genre, in form—free-verse lines centering on four stresses, but casually so—and its three long periods felt like a physical deformity of my own that I had to live with. But in its association for me now with the dream of the Trumpeter, and with the poem which claimed, elicited, misinterpreted it (or whatever) it has settled into a new kind of place for me. The "night mirror" is both mirror and lamp, reflecting, cold satellite moon of night vision and sun of informing light, that appears at the end of the poem in a mediating position between planet and pillow, both within and beyond the sleeper-waker's head. It is the mimetic-expressive mirror of my own imagination, and a frightening one; the image of "the head of the bed" was born in that poem, although I would not know it until long after its rebirth as the title (added after composition of all fifteen sections) of the later poem. "The Night Mirror" was a parable about the relation of poem and dream which I wrote for my own instruction at the time, and if it fell among thorns at first, it eventually worked its way down to good ground.

Writing this now, I have come to see that the parable could not have been explicit at the time. I was just beginning in those years to read Spenser with *poetic* seriousness, and beginning to understand how *The Interpretation of Dreams*—surely one of the greatest works of criticism in our age—was making the quality of dream available for serious poetic consideration. I mean by this that any earnest, modernist literary aspirant of the 1950s, told in impressionistic, belle-lettristic essays that Spenser's world of faerie had the glory and the freshness of the land of dreams, would fling such essays aside with an oath, convinced that the quality of dream for such a writer meant imprecision, flight from signification, botched mimesis, steam filling the lower half of a Dali-like set in a bad movie, and so forth. Freud's masterpiece in fact treated dreams as if they were as serious as poems, and thereby made the notion of dream serious enough to be likened, by a conceptual adult, to poetry, without invoking all of the qualities that one knew poetry, as opposed to sentimental bad writing, always had to shun.

In any event, the text-dream relation in my earlier poem was a trope for the imagination: that much I have understood for some time. In a poem of the spring of 1974 (written some months after the publication in chapbook form of "The Head of the Bed") called "The Train" I worked some of the landscape from recurring dreams of my own and of my wife of twenty years from whom I was just then separated; it was as if perhaps to augment imagination's power over events it could only represent. "The Train" concerns two fictional dreamers, lying beside each other in bed, dreaming overlapping—or, in the mythology of the poem, interpenetrating—dreams. Actual dreams of transportation systems, missed connections and of a particular, unique dream which had in fact recently been "shared" by two sleepers in bed together—these composed the scenery of various episodes in the poem, which were connected by continuing glimpses of a train—the train of the poem's thought—making its way through a larger landscape. Sometimes, in a tunnel, it became the actual sexual penetration of one of the sleepers by the other, and similarly one dream "inside" another one. That railroad ties are called "sleepers" provides another mode of connection between the metaphoric train and the dreamers in and around the poem.

I don't think that I could have managed "The Train" (a poem

which I prize highly) without having come to terms with the meta-rela-
tion, as it were, of three relations between dream and text: (1) allusion to
actual dreams of one's own, (2) narrative fictions of dreaming in the text,
and (3) the condition of poetry (or genre of poem, if one must, or intensity of poetic force) which allows a poetic text, no matter how carefully
contrived and constructed, to escape from the hand of the poet's wit, and
partake of the unwitting poesis of dream work. Poems are neither night-
dream nor day-dream, which is something the ambiguous nationality of
the Trumpeter may be asserting.

It was only having to comment on the trumpeting dream that
occasioned my reassessment of it, of the whole poem to which it was
added, and of "The Night Mirror." I realize now that in these remarks I
have been treating that early poem as a kind of inner vocation. It is only
having gone along so far in reconstructing that leads me back again to the
meaning of the later parable I told myself, the parable of the Trumpeter.
Theirs or ours? Sleeping or waking? I now read it as a fable of what trope
is, of where its home is, travel widely though it may; a fable not of the sea
of figure as opposed to the literal shore, but of a division made at right
angles to the coastline, as it were, by which what lay on either side the
boundary would look identical.

But I now see something else as well. Sleep has a brother kingdom, and the trumpeter of trope, the music of representation, plays at the
boundary of Death and Life in this wise: fictions, the lies we tell ourselves
to avert the continuing and otherwise paralyzing gaze of death, the way
in which those fictions lie not against truth so much as against time, must
ultimately serve the cause of Life. But perhaps, in another kind of
tromperie dernière, they may actually be in the employ of Death, whose
ultimate victory may be augmented by the loss of any intervening apparent battles. Is our imagination, then, brave or pitiable? No one can ever
know whether the Trumpeter is theirs or ours.

DAVID IGNATOW

Born in Brooklyn on the eve of World War I, David
Ignatow published fifteen volumes of poetry and several of prose before his death in 1997. His memoir,
The One in the Many, came out in 1988, and a sub-
stantial collection of his poems, *Against the Evidence:
Selected Poems, 1934–1994*, appeared in 1995. Ignatow taught at the New School for Social Research,
New York University, and Columbia University, and
won the Bollingen Prize and the National Institute
of Arts and Letters Award.

THE DREAM AND THE BAGEL

write in a dreamlike state, the experience all creative artists share. One such experience for me has become a widely anthologized poem, "The Bagel," and from its acceptance and my pleasure in writing it, discovering for myself a new process in the making of a poem, I have taken it as my standard for subsequent poems.

The fact, though, is that I can't quite grasp how that particular dream came into existence for me. I don't believe I willed it. It's not possible to will such an image into one's consciousness, because it would assume that there was a prior recognition of it. That was not the case. However, I can recall the process piecemeal and factually.

I was consumed by a sense of limitations, and it saddened me to have to acknowledge that I was not going to achieve all I had hoped for myself. It was given me to accept this condition and to acknowledge it, but in order to do so I needed to express outwardly and accurately my capacity to live with my limitations. They were not only my personal shortcomings but also those I observed and was living through in the world. I was seated at my desk beneath a window in broad daylight and thinking these thoughts.

It suddenly struck me that I had grasped my problem in an objective mode. In objectivity having found the means of distancing myself from immersion in the self, I began to see it humorously. I knew from the past how humor had relieved me of strain in other circumstances of tension and it would be humor with a decided bias towards the familiar in my life, such as gripes towards meals that were not fulfilling or lacking in taste. I could be humorously nasty about such things. And yet there were foods I enjoyed under most any circumstance, such as ice cream, ham and eggs, bacon, lox and bagel. For some reason, at that moment, I grasped onto the bagel as an image with which to write humorously of my sad understanding and acceptance of the shortcomings in my life, and I found myself enjoying the idea of a bagel as an image of limitation in its circumscribed roundness, with a metaphorical hole in the middle. By dropping the bagel, I would be acknowledging my having dropped from me whatever hopes I had for myself and for the world I lived in.

I in the image of a bagel, circumscribed as was the bagel by its size and shape—the humor of it touched me to imagine further the adventures of a bagel round and smooth suggesting a wheel and thus find myself, as a bagel, rolling head over heels across the ground and not unhappy with myself, affirmed in myself in my condition and enjoying it.

Subsequently, I have ventured further in my dreamlike state during the day, at my typewriter, and have invented situations without basis in reality that approximate a night dream. Actual night dreams escape me the moment I arouse myself from sleep to write them down. I invent as the mood strikes me, exactly as I experience it during sleep. Whether I am inventing legitimate dreams in my waking dreamlike state is a question I often ask myself, but at the same time I realize that my method must in some form or fashion resemble the process of symbolist writing, though not surrealist, as many dreams seem to be.

I'm quite satisfied with my daytime adaptation of the dream state at night. In fact, after completing a poem invented without basis in reality, I am as satisfied and fulfilled in my invention as I can recall my experience with actual night dreams, from which I awaken at times pleasantly and at other times depressed, depending upon the dream. I can do all that and more with my waking method, to my satisfaction. In my dreamlike state, I am capable of guiding the poem through its growth and form, something I cannot do with my night dreams. And so, for my own purposes, I am quite happy with my method and rather proud that while I may be writing from anger, frustration or weakness, it is what gives me an affirmation of my self, after all.

The Bagel

I stopped to pick up the bagel
rolling away in the wind,
annoyed with myself
for having dropped it
as if it were a portent.
Faster and faster it rolled,
with me running after it
bent low, gritting my teeth,
and I found myself doubled over
and rolling down the street
head over heels, one complete somersault
after another like a bagel
and strangely happy with myself.

ROBERT KELLY

Robert Kelly has long been associated with the writing program at Bard College, where he continues his own prolific writing career. Since his first collection, *Armed Descent,* appeared in 1961, he has published over fifty volumes of poetry and fiction, including *The Common Shore* (1969), *Flesh Dream Book* (1971), and more recently, *Red Actions: Selected Poems, 1960–1993* (Black Sparrow, 1995). This most anti-Establishment of poets was honored in 1994 with the degree of Doctor of Letters by the State University of New York.

SEVENTEEN ARCANA FROM THE INFINITY OF DREAMS

I.

For a poet to write about dreams is like a man trying to describe his wife. Nothing he ever says can possibly do justice to her beauty, sustaining wisdom, intimate knowledge, and her sheer importance to him in every aspect of his life.

Nothing I can say will reveal the profound yet simple otherness from which we wake, every single day of our lives, wordlessly instructed to begin anew. To tell afresh.

And yet the man must again and again try to tell about his wife. He tries to describe the actuality, fullness, of her. Only to find himself reduced to telling mere anecdotes about her, stories that his listeners may find silly or pointless or incomprehensible. Just so, the poet begins by writing vastly about Dream, and winds up by telling a dream or two. Telling a dream, then, may be a little like showing a snapshot of your wife . . .

Dream—is it synecdoche? A part from which we must, by divine or mathematic cunning, intuit a whole?

2.

My dream, we say.

As if a dream is mine—
and perhaps it is.

Maybe my dream is the only thing in the world that is truly mine.

Since my body belongs just as much to you.

3.

How we speak of dreams, how we claim them, or let them claim us.

Dr. King said: "I have a dream"—but that kind of dream is the precise opposite of the dream that comes to us in the night. Dr. King's dream is a daytime vision of compassion and order and renewal. It is a vision.

Yet the power of his great cry! How much of that power comes from his use of the apparently simple word, "dream"? Isn't the dream the thing that comes in the night and masters us? And mastering us, it gives to its declaration, its vision, an air of the prophetic. Since it comes from the dark, from the Gods, it comes to us with an authenticity greater than anything we might merely want, even if we want it with all our hearts.

4.

What is Dream, what is Vision?

Do you say: I dreamt of you
or
I had a dream of you?

Do they mean different things?

5.

Can you tell a real dream from an invented dream? Is there a difference between a dream that comes along to someone in the night, and a dream that is made up by the same someone in the daytime—invented (according to the usual hypothesis) by the same mind that dreamed the "real" dream?

Is it possible that all our narratives, fictions, lies, daydreams are nothing but dreams ill-silenced by the light of day, creations dimly remembered from within the chambers of the night, but no longer insulated by sleep?

6.

Where does a dream live in time?

I notice that some people tell their dreams in the present tense ("I'm walking down this hallway, and there's this figure coming towards me, I can't see its face, it's hooded . . .") and some people tell their dreams in the past tense ("I was on a beach in some southern place, Spain, maybe, and I looked out to sea and a woman was walking in towards the shore. I could see her only in silhouette . . .")

When a dream is told in the present tense: the dreamer is still experiencing the dream, still at the mercy of the dream negotiation.

Negotium perambulans in tenebris: the business that walketh about in the night, the Bible said. What we used to call the "progressive" aspect, action going on simultaneously with its description. The dream told in the present tense is happening now.

When a dream is told in the past tense: the dreamer has distanced himself from the dream. The dreamer is trying to assert control.

Narration is control.

That's the absolute of it. Past tense narration asserts absolute control. Control is safety. The teller is safe from the tale, safe from the told.

On the other hand, the present tense narration is still in flux, it can change, the dream can change, squirm in the dreamer's grasp, become a different thing.

Or is the dream always a different thing?

The Jungians play at wakeful dreaming. Once the analyst Nor Hall and I found ourselves at a party holding each other by our living waists as we danced one strange summer dawn and I thought: neither by sleep nor intention did this strange dream come into the world of flesh, this world we call actual, but by the way things work out. Karma. Or, *la vida es* indeed *sueño*. Neither of us planned it, neither of us told it, yet it held us, firmly in its grasp. We happened to each other, for those few minutes, the way dream happens to us.

8.
Dreams are just the parts of sleep we notice. Life is just the part we notice of all that's going on. It's all we dare sign our name to. Life is the part of existence we feel we have the right to complain about.

Alive and kicking, as they say.

9.
Dream is so much less a mystery than anything else that happens. Maybe dream is the simplest thing of all that happens.

Just the mind, alone in the night.

No body, but it feels. No body, but it moves. So simple. So few its needs.

10.
Why don't we need as little as a dream does?

It needs so little to do its work.

What is the work of dream?

(We know what Freud called the dream work, but that's what we propose to do with it. We want to make it show us something we think it knows. Twisting the arm of a dream.)

But what is the dream's own work? What does it want with us? What does it do with us?

Well, as Freud also pointed out, it wakes us up.

It returns us to the place where we wake and breed and work and die, and a new generation of dreamers takes our place.

11.

Remember the cartoon showing Goldilocks as a sweet old lady, reminiscing to her grandchildren: "Well, I never dreamed that there were *bears* living in that house . . ."

To dream here means to have a foretaste of the actual, as well as of what comes. Who might be living in that woodsy house? What might be waiting for us inside the radiant precincts of the coming day? Who, right now, is on the other side of the door? Who is inside your eyes?

12.

The way we use the word. "I have a dream"—but that means nothing born of the night, but born of conscious wit and will gazing into that vast somber scary thing called the future. Dr. King filled that dark with the lightning flash of his motivation to heal his people. Truly call him Doctor King. But scarcely a dreamer, though he had a dream.

13.
The way we use the words.

I never dreamt . . .
I never dream.

I have a dream . . .
I had a dream . . .

I dream of Miriam who . . .
(And in my father's day they used to call a fancied lover a . . . dream boat
. . . but you don't need one to sail to Dreamland.)

They say that dream comes from an Old English word that meant "joy."
Such pleasure is hard to stand.

We tell our dream to a doctor. The doctor is trained to digest this information without being destroyed by it. A dream is dangerous.

So if somebody wants to tell you their dream, lie down on the couch or
the ground and compose yourself as if to sleep, close your eyes and listen.
I used to run a dream workshop and that's what we did. We pretended to
our bodies that we were sleeping, so that when the person told the dream
she had "had," we could seem to be dreaming it too. That is the best way
to hear a dream—to dream it along with the dreamer. That is the richest
way. That is also the safest way, the body snug in its posture of listening
inward, safe from the arrogant mind.

14.

Judgment is later, and interpretation, and all those energetic dances of the mind with its images. Dance with your images, darling, they're all you have.

Interpretation. Of course I interpret dreams when I am told them. Seldom when I have them. I do not often dream.

15.

Dream = spontaneously recall the dream at waking or soon after.

That's what we really mean (socially, linguistically) by dreaming.

That's what she means when she wakes him in the morning and asks: Did you dream?

Dreaming means then: remembering *now* an experience *then*. What a strangely simple doctrine of Time we must cherish, to be so easy with Then and Now. From within the walls of sleep we carry something with us.

16.

Evidently what we call dreaming is a kind of remembering.

Not every morning, nothing is certain, I am listening to Schumann—the *Symphonic Etudes* that Pat Meanor gave me, played by Jean-Yves Thibaudet—and thinking about dream. Then I begin to think about Schumann—the tragedy of his invariant attention, the hopeless grandeur of his ardor, the intensity of his devotion, the radiant tonality of his desperate refusal to despair. But then an end came even to that, to him; one morning the dream just does not come.

There is such grandeur in the world, such goodness, if we wake to find it, let it find us. But nothing is certain, the right hand moves at a different speed from the left hand, they make a beautiful music, that is true, that may last, if not forever, still last long enough for us to hear it.

Does the dream last long enough for us to tell it?

And if we do not tell it, what is the dream then?

And whose dream is it then?

Is there something, anything, in our world that is not told?

17.
When I was a little boy I learned that everything is better after sleep, everything is better in the morning.

I have never truly decided whether it is the sleeping or the waking that heals.
But healing certainly there is, between the last flutter of despondent weariness and the first wink of daylight.

Of course I suppose now it is the dream that heals us.

But I suspect that the dream we do not remember is the dream that heals us. Instead, it   re-members us, and we wake healed.

FAYE KICKNOSWAY

Faye Kicknosway was born in Detroit but, as she puts it, "did a lot of her growing up in Portland and L.A." A Woodrow Wilson Fellowship took her to San Francisco and an important teacher, Nanos Valaoritis. Other early influences include Ben Hecht, S. J. Perelman, George Trakl, and Ted Berrigan. In the mid-1980s, after eight books, an NEA, and a Pulitzer Prize nomination, she "took a one semester Visiting Distinguished Writer gig at the University of Hawaii at Manoa, and, like *The Man Who Came to Dinner*, stayed." Her works include *A Man Is a Hook. Trouble* (1974), and *All These Voices: New and Selected Poems* (1986). She is also an accomplished graphic artist. Her work, both visual and literary, has always been startling, as one can see from the following essay, which combines the scholarly and the hallucinatory.

INSIDE OUT

for Shirley Ruth

magining how dream comes to my page is like looking through a series of Mylar cels, each surfaced with disparate, animated subject matter. The process of dreaming—which dreaming?: night, and that varied and layered; or day, which is constant and sometimes suspends, augments, embellishes the finite structure the "I" tunnels through.

Revery; there are no bones in my hand, just fairy tales and movie stars. Whatever I touch, isn't, and I, touching, am not. What shape, thing, moment endures except as memory which also erodes? I watch a man fall down the side of a building on a rope: a window washer. He is the same size as the gnat on the screen. I know he is his own size and that if he saw me, I would be the gnat. I raise my glass mug of tea; he swings out above its rim, descends, polishes its glass wall, falls lower, is in the tea, swinging out from his rope, his arm extending, moving. There are no ripples, no bubbles on the tea's surface to evidence his descent toward the bottom of the mug, nor can I see him, only his rope and that momentarily static, then moving from side to side as he gets a purchase with his feet on the next section of glass to clean.

When does the dream not enter the page? As Mickey Spillane or Eudora Welty it cannot be kept from the page, which is its seed pod. The eye above, a hive of images, follows the pen's delicious incision. And it is Buñuel: the eye and moon sliced open; an escape of ants from a crucified palm.

As performance artist Justin Chin once said, "A dream is nothing until you wake up." Then he loaned me a book called *Maps to Anywhere*. It could have been a scene in a dream instead of *Just Desserts* in San Francisco: the male figure, more Jungian than Freudian, tells you, the novice, the seeker, an important, encoded sentence that you must remember when you wake up, and hands you a mysterious object, or book, that will unlock you from whatever restraint that keeps you entrapped in a cave of ignorant behavior, freeing you magically into luminous thought and action.

The architecture of a dream; its weight; its narrative; the eye shifts; it's one of Magritte's windows, the landscape beyond it broken glass scattered on the floor beneath the window sill and at the foot of an easel upon which is a painting of what the landscape was. Or perhaps what the landscape, which is a black, empty hole, wishes to become. Perhaps time has passed. The pieces of broken glass were once clear. Now they echo parts of the painted landscape, but in disarray. It will take centuries for the glass to fit itself together. Will it be leaded and lit as though from a light outside it? Will it add angels and saints, be Tintoretto or Poussin? Perhaps Cézanne or Turner? A dream is metamorphosis, integration, accident. As Joseph Cornell said: " . . . distinct from perspective."

In a file, I have a newspaper article concerning the mysterious deaths of young, male Pacific Islanders. They die in their sleep in the throes of a violent dream. Females of all ages, very young boys and old men are immune to the dream; only warrior age young men die. It's called the Sleeping Sickness and when it hits, the male populations of villages are almost wiped out. There's no rescue; the sleeper cannot be awakened and saved. Once the dream begins, the dreamer is lost. It is a different relationship to the word "nothing" in Justin's reference to dream. Is dying from a dream another way of waking up from it? If you die while you're dreaming, do you stay in the dream? Are you caught there in whatever scene, in combination with whatever object, forever? What does that make of the air we breathe if it's so? Does our breathing distort, perhaps free, the trapped dreamers? And if so, what becomes of them?

Geza Roheim, in *The Gates of the Dream*, said sleep is the womb and too much like death to make us happy to go there. The dream is the father's penis, its ejaculate what we abscond into sleep to remind us that we are alive. There is one basic dream all people of the earth have, and four primary dream patterns, only three of which I can remember. He also wrote: "Her vagina is a tomato," a sentence I immediately copied into a notebook. Falling, being chased, being somehow contained in an enclosure, like a room, a box, an oven, or a car, are the three dream patterns I remember. Flying, a dream I have attempted and failed at at least twice is not one of the four. It is the dollop of mayonnaise on a sandwich or, closer to Roheim, the slice of pickle on the plate beside the sandwich.

What I have dreamed my entire life is not a pattern dream, either: I'm traveling; I have a destination; I never get there. Whatever the accoutrements of the dream, whether I am in open country by a fence, stalled, considering going over or under it, or I open a door onto a hallway where corpses are tied to a wall, or I step down, having shouldered the clothing aside, from a dark closet to a busy city street, I continue my journey. I might be slowed down, but I am never stopped, except by waking up. Then I am tied to a clock. Am I the oil painting or the broken glass, assembling? Have I left "real time" and entered *Alcheringa,* the "dreamtime"? That's what Australian Bushmen believe. The brief, physical world of the accumulating past is what is not real, what is awakened from.

Which brings me back to Roheim and his work in the Arnhem Islands. There are three bodies each of us have, the physical body, the spirit body, and the soul. The latter two get out of the first during sleep and wander about. If an enemy moves the physical body from where it fell asleep, the other two cannot find their way back to it, and it lingers, asleep, then dies. St. Teresa of Avila experienced catalepsy more than once in her life and was presumed dead and laid out for burial, and awoke, and either climbed or was lifted down from her bier, much to the amazement of her mourners. Her physical body, moved from where it had fallen asleep, must have had a voice loud as a foghorn to call the two wanderers back. Duns Scotus wasn't so lucky. His wanderers found him already buried. Duns Scotus did not become a saint because of the disposition of his body in his coffin when he was disinterred. He had been thrashing around in it. There were gouges in the lid as though he had been trying to claw his way through it. A saint would not do that, it was reckoned, and he was nailed closed and reburied. I forget the name of the saint who had a wonderfully incorruptible body. He looked like he was sleeping, until someone, wanting a relic to take back home with him, cut a finger off the saint's marvelous body, and blood rushed out of the hole the absent finger left—or so the story says—and the body shriveled and decayed before the thief's astonished eyes. Someone once said that on the day of judgment, those on their way to heaven had better duck because of the kneecaps, fingers, teeth, femurs flying through the air from wherever they've been kept as relics, so the saints can, so to speak, reassemble themselves before they meet their Maker.

Perhaps this is what will happen to my poems. Lines will disappear, phrases, commas, in a rush, whole stanzas, the idea underlying a poem, its mood, intent, everything I've harvested from dreams, not only my dreams; I admit I am a dream thief, not as bad as the thief in Capote's story; I don't take them all; just a piece; it's more like archeology; a shard; a fragment; up it will all go; collecting and collective; a pantheon; a nebula. Entire books, like termite wings, will disintegrate. No more "Who Shall Know Them?" because, although it was Walker Evans's photographs I worked from, it was a dream that fueled the work. Like Faulkner's little girl in the pear tree, it never got spoken on the page. But it will, I believe, in the interconnected poems I have begun, where it is the visible adhesive between the various sections that have no body yet, only the yearning, despair and anger at the heart of the dream.

"Heart"? Why not "crotch" or "larynx"? The body of the dream; which parts of it do we, upon awakening, find in our mouths? Does the dream, broken into, pilfered, decay? Or does it seal itself closed, regenerate the missing part, immune to mortality, infinitely alive?

Boris Karloff as Stevenson's body snatcher, what he pulled up and fed through the basement door to medical students. Coldly, villainously, and with death-ever-after waiting for him. But he had no dreams, the body snatcher; he was a void the bodies passed through becoming landscape for medical students to map.

Centuries earlier, da Vinci had donned the role of grave robber and could have been food for crows if he had been caught while acting it. His notebooks very probably would have been destroyed. What else of his might have been erased by church and state because of the sacrilege he committed? Why did he do it? It must have been a kick because he knew he would be tortured and killed if he were caught. Where did he cut them up, his delicious cadavers? How did he keep from being found out? He was no conduit as was the Karloff character; he harvested for himself and could not walk away—free—money in his pocket, the door closed, the night's work accomplished. His work was his notebooks, everything else was simply preparation. The so precise drawings of the pancreas, the spleen were not meant for anyone to see, were not "art" to him; da Vinci didn't give a hoot about art. His résumé was long. Grave robbing was not on it and "painter" was an oh-by-the-way near the bottom of the list of what he could do. What must it have been like for him slicing open his first corpse and there, in full color, were the viscera of the dead animals that littered his world: man as dog, as chicken; not as "in God's Image." Had he expected stars? The plants of Eden? Or had he already seen and perhaps touched with his foot his first eviscerated man: torture victim, war dead, famine, pestilence? He considered himself an inventor of armaments and sold himself as such to whatever court would hire him. Two hundred years before the word came into language, he was a scientist. Why didn't he paint what he found in the human body? Why only drawings? Accuracy was what he practiced. Why not the color of the pancreas, of fat? He felt himself to be a failure. Painting was dalliance, distraction; it kept him from what he wanted to do. The airplane, the tank, the helicopter, pulled from his dreaming, stayed in his notebooks along with the internal organs he had fished out of their cave into the air and ink of the page.

Dream; as in Cinderella's milk-tooth song: Snow White's; or Jiminy Cricket's: the miracle of wood to flesh? As in the sneer, "In your dreams." Or, good old practical mom always worried you will not have a life beyond the horror of your collecting stupidity: "Stop your daydreaming."

My grandmother called it "woolgathering." I thought, Sheep? Glenn Ford? Cowboys murdering shepherds? I saw myself with a rag-picker's bag over my shoulder, in my hand a stick with a sharp point, someone from Dickens, Edward Gorey's "Hapless Child," flailing the stick at the blowing fuzz from blankets, stacks of them like coal in a factory yard, piled all around me. There was an electrified barbed wire fence and Nazis in guard towers. My life; I was a woolgatherer, doomed to black and white; Alec Guinness as Disraeli couldn't save me; no one could.

A woman, perhaps Ava Gardner, technicolor, sits at a dressing table combing her hair with a fish. Her arm moves slowly and although there is a large round mirror behind the perfume bottles on the dressing table, she is looking into an oval mirror she holds up by its stem before her face, her expression captured and intensified in its smaller surface, seductive, sensual, as though she were looking at her lover. The one observing her shifts his gaze, for it seems to be a man, the scene should be black and white, *Gilda,* Rita Hayworth, but it is not a curtained window beyond the dressing table, rather, opened terrace doors. It is night. There is the noise of bombs exploding, artillery fire, machine guns, screaming. The observer listens; it is violins to him; he is content. He slips his left hand into his trouser pocket. I see his black evening clothes, the silk lapels, the stiff white collar and bow tie at his throat. He has no head. I can look down from his neck at the floor, the toes of his shiny black shoes, or across his shoulders, to the left or the right. I can look from the back of his collar to the lighted hallway beyond the open door he has just stepped through. I am not him and can move invisibly, freely around the room, an amorphous voyeur.

It's a skill I've had both awake and asleep since childhood when I could disappear into my eyes as dumb as an animal or a tree. There was no "I," only a field of moving light particles. It had nothing to do with concentration, focus, attention; nothing at all. Those are directed, imposed. It had to do with sickness. I forget when I read Huxley's two works, "The Doors of Perception" and "Heaven and Hell," but it was a kick; the naming of the first eleven years of my life.

Huxley used mescaline and lysergic acid in a clinical setting with an investigator because he was looking for "The Door in the Wall," Blake's and other visionaries' experiencing of the world. It led him to readings in physiology, in history, especially concerning privation: what the brain does when it is bereft of nutrients because the body is starving for one reason or another: famine, plague, ascetic practice. Food, the lack of, a blight on—in Salem, the devil came from ergot on the heads of the rye plants; it was his body the people ate as bread, saw, with held breath, leaning in through the window; which was their eyes; and he leaned out from them; their bellies aboil with his adrenalin. The body and food; when there isn't any, like Zosimus, the body eats itself, and from that activity, lifts out of itself, is no-self, no "it," is act without subject. I was born with a sixteen-inch appendix coiled around a portion of my intestines. The first eleven years of my life were hallucinated because my body simply could not process food. I had high fevers, vomited what I ate, passed out a lot. A vice-principal brought me home from school, exasperated that I had to be continually scooped up off the hallway floors and taken to her or the nurse's office. She said I was not to return to school until whatever was wrong with me was fixed. Surgically it was, and my mother was told I would have a more or less "normal" life if I made it past eighteen. I've often wondered which "eighteen"; there seems always to be another shelf of them I haven't found yet, put down the toilet, thrown in the garbage, vacuumed up, burned.

I sometimes think dream is a state I live in, enter at its whim, and dip back into when I work. I don't know what I would have been if I hadn't been sick as a child. My life is lit by those early years, and the "act" of being alive is the movement, like meeting death coming through the mirror in *Orphée*, of the two worlds as hermaphrodite: one body, conscious, unconscious, fused, sometimes remembering, sometimes forgetting. Dream is the parent Bachelard speaks of in his book about Lautréamont: what is real is the imagination, the invisible that is always making this, where we sit, up.

Instead of Jimmy Cagney, spraddle-legged, guns blazing—"Whaddaya know; whaddaya say?"—I was Caspar Hauser—"I want to be a horseman"—cast up to a sunlit city street, gone the cellar stones, our humming and bleating, our shape shifting. I was a kazoo, a stick of gum, period, the end. Walls were solids and no longer spoke to me. I was only in one place; there weren't three of me walking through chairs and doors and each other. I could stop myself from passing out by tapping my fingers steadily against the center of my forehead. The inside was locked down, only brief moments of it escaping, unexpectedly, for the next ten years: a classmate's shoulder would catch fire with a brilliant white light, and I would be obliterated; or a pebble on the sidewalk would leap up from where it had been and radiate a ferocious light that moved and was alive.

My mother began to worry about my future. She wanted me to teach art to children, go and live in the second grade where nobody ever got fired, and parents loved you, and all you had to do was make papier-mâché animals all day. It was her dream that I be safe from whatever dangerous thing I was dreaming up for myself. Ridley Scott's *Alien* did not exist yet, but she had seen me watch it move across the room. Just as my brother, later, watched it, until it killed him.

I once knew a guy who said he dreamed, pretty regularly, the same dream. He was falling from a cliff, sometimes a tree, a roof, it varied, toward a coiled rattlesnake that was ready to strike him before he touched the ground. The snake was an embellishment to one of Roheim's basic dream patterns, and I told him. He said, "Fuck that psychiatrist shit. I know the snake hits me, I'm dead, kaput, finito. I don't need no gobbledegook shrink tell me what my dream means; I know. I'm gonna die in my sleep, and my stupid fuck son'll say, 'He died so peaceful; in his sleep,' and he'll *believe* it. Let me tell you, I'd rather have my left nut cut off than dream that dream. There's nothing worse happens in life than that dream. I wake up, every hair on my body's standing straight up, like I'm a goddam porcupine."

He collected old radio shows and I vaguely remember the ending of one of them, an *Inner Sanctum*, I think. A narrator is alone in an old house, scared out of his wits. There's a maniacal sound of an old woman laughing, first at a distance, then closer and closer, until she's right in front of him. She doesn't talk, only laughs. The narrator is frantic. The old woman's voice is suddenly muffled. She's still laughing, but it's like she's inside a rubber glove. There's a wet squish. She's turned inside out. The narrator screams. The sound of his running feet. His final, hysterical "No, No!" and his voice muffles, disappears. The sound of a wet rubber glove being turned inside out. The final squish. Silence. Then the climactic, full-shriek music. Then silence, broken by the announcer, what happens next week; the commercial; the end; which is what this is.

MAXINE KUMIN

VICTOR KUMIN

In her long career, Maxine Kumin has won acclaim as poet, novelist, essayist, and children's writer. Her many books of poetry include *The Nightmare Factory* (1970), the Pulitzer Prize–winning *Up Country* (1972), *Our Ground Time Here Will Be Brief* (1982), and *Looking For Luck* (1992). More recent volumes include *Connecting the Dots* (1996) and *Selected Poems, 1960–1990* (1997). Prose works include *Women, Animals, and Vegetables: Essays and Stories* (1994). She won the 1995 Aiken Prize, served as poetry consultant to the Library of Congress, and is currently a chancellor of the Academy of American Poets. A dedicated rider and driver of horses, Kumin lives with her husband on a farm in Warner, New Hampshire.

SCRUBBED UP AND SENT TO SCHOOL

"**S**ubduing the Dream in Alaska," a poem I wrote some years ago, opens with a statement in which I have implicit faith:

> In the visiting poet's workshop
> the assignment is to write down a dream.
> The intent, before the week is out,
> is to show how much a poem is like
> a dream set straight, made rational.
> A dream scrubbed up and sent to school.

I've had good luck with this assignment in my own classes eliciting far-ranging and unexpected material. The results in the prison workshop led me to make a statement about our role in the Native American culture, a statement I had not foreseen as the subject of the poem. The wonderful thing about starting with dream content is the unpredictability of the outcome. While many of my dreams are too bizarre (sexual, scatological or fragmentary) to serve as springboards, a goodly number have announced themselves as wanting further waking work, and several have risen up into completed poems.

Risen up, as mushrooms do, I have written, in "The Dreamer, the Dream," searching in my frustration to recapture an elusive dream's content:

> After the sleeper has burst his night pod
> climbed up out of its silky holdings
> the dream must stumble alone now . . .
>
> In search of some phantom outcome
> while on both sides of the tissue
> the dreamer walks into the weather . . .

> . . . and in fact he comes
> upon a great cluster of honey mushrooms . . .
>
> lumbering from their dark fissure
> going up like a dream going on.

How often do we carry around with us the setting, the situation, the encounter, unable, it seems to break free from it? This was precisely what happened to the dream encounter in "My Father's Neckties." In hopes of coming to terms with this ghostly reunion that nagged me through an entire day, I sat down to write it out:

> Last night my color-blind chainsmoking father
> who has been dead for fourteen years
> stepped up out of a basement tie shop
> downtown and did not recognize me.

Twenty lines later, the significance of our meeting "where we had loved each other, keeping it quiet," announced itself. The giant father of my childhood was indeed

> . . . a man who wore hard colors recklessly
> and hid out in the foreign
> bargain basements of his feelings.

To this day I reexperience that sense of closure, even of liberation, upon seeing the metaphor that had driven both the dream and the poem.

While my brother was dying of ALS (Lou Gehrig's disease), I had a succession of vivid premonitory dreams about him, the early ones rich with denial, the later ones horrific in their acceptance. Just after his doctor had arrived at a definitive diagnosis (a death sentence), my unconscious recreated my brother:

Tonight he strides in rosy-cheeked
and eighteen in the pectorals
to announce he has six months to live and plans
for every hour. . . .
           Further, he means to kill
time with a perpetual-motion cell.

That last detail is both tragic and funny. My brother, a skilled engineer, had from early childhood been a lively tinkerer, taking clocks and toasters, electric shavers and vacuum cleaners apart, sometimes reassembling them for their betterment. It was logical for the dreaming mind to envisage a way out, a perpetual-motion cell that would arrest time and with it the inexorable forward movement of the disease.

As his condition became more evident, my dream self began to come to terms with the inevitable.

Listen! I love you!
I've always loved you!
And so we totter and embrace
. . . saying our goodbyes. . . .

in a downtown parking garage, this far a direct account of an evening all four of us, with our spouses, had spent together at dinner and theater. But I was in no way prepared for the content of the dream that followed what I intuited was to be our final outing as a family:

At 3 A.M. I'm driven to such extremes
that when the sorrowing hangman
brings me your severed penis still
tumescent from the scaffold
yet dried and pressed as faithfully
as a wildflower
I put it away on my closet shelf
and lie back down in my lucky shame.

My immediate association, odd though it seems, is to John Crowe Ransom's "Piazza Piece":

> But what grey man among the vines is this
> Whose words are dry and faint as in a dream?
> Back from my trellis, Sir, before I scream!

In this perfect Petrarchan sonnet, youth and age, the life force and death are represented as the "lady young in beauty" and the "gentleman in a dustcoat." The latter emblem emerges in my dream as the actual killer, the hangman. I can't defend against the image of the tumescent penis, except to say that folklore holds that the hanged victim experiences an erection upon strangulation. (My brother was at that time having difficulty in speaking and swallowing. It was plain to see what was coming next.) In the dream I am awarded this token of the life force. I put it away as one would any other treasure "and lie back down in my lucky shame"—ashamed to be still alive, lucky with the treasure of my own existence even as his is taken from him.

Reading through my early poems I am taken aback by the presence in them of so much dream material, so much detail "scrubbed up and sent to school" to make, for better or worse, the whole poem. My reverence for the unconscious is with me still, although I remember fewer dreams and am pricked less often by the recollected fragments into working them into poems. Almost invariably, the dreams-into-poems have involved family members or very close friends.

"The Longing to Be Saved," a series of recurrent nightmares while I was housed in a motel in Fayetteville, Arkansas, one February, began: "When the barn catches fire / I am wearing the wrong negligee." The next segment dealt with rescuing my children, then my mother, and lastly my husband, who was home on the farm in New Hampshire during this wintry season when house fires are an ever-present threat ("I hold the rope as you slide from danger"). The poem ends with this curious reversal: "Now the family's out, there's no holding back. / I go in to get my turn."

Although the resolution seems appropriate to the poem and solves the puzzle of the title, it baffles me as much now as it did during the composition. How could I dream myself running back (much as the horses do, in the opening stanza) into the flaming house? And are we allowed to astonish ourselves with a poem's closure? These questions must go unanswered.

But no dreams have been as vivid or lingered as long as the ones that haunted me after the suicide of my best friend and fellow poet, Anne Sexton. For seventeen years we communicated daily, if not face-to-face then by local or long-distance telephone. From "Splitting Wood at Six Above":

> . . . I'm still
> talking to you (last night's dream);
> we'll split the phone bill.
> It's expensive calling
> from the other side

through "Progress Report":

> Dear friend, last night I dreamed
> you held a sensitive position,
> you were Life's Counselor
> coming to the phone in Vaud or Bern,
> some terse one-syllable place,
> to tell me how to carry on. . . .

the loss is acute and the desire to reestablish contact (unsurprisingly, by phone) is urgent. These dreams, and others unrecorded, occurring in the first year or two following her death, find me not so much bereft as bewildered, not so angry as made desolate by the loss of our daily exchanges.

As time passed I was gradually able, I think, to express anger as well as sorrow. In "Itinerary of an Obsession," written perhaps a year, perhaps two years later than "Progress Report," Sexton turns up in a series of dream montages. In the first of these,

> . . . here you come
> leaping out of the coffin again,
> flapping around the funeral home
> crying Surprise! I was only fooling!

It's a bizarre scene that refers, I think, to the numerous half-hearted suicide attempts Sexton had made before the actual event and seeks to reflect the mixture of relief and helpless fury the rescuer feels in this situation. In the next frame, in Rome at St. Peter's Square:

> when the pope comes to the window . . .
> you turn up arranging to receive
> extreme unction from an obliging priest
> with a bad cold. You swivel your head
> to keep from inhaling his germs.

The association with Catholicism is not accidental; Anne was drawn to the Church, strongly attracted to its ritual and longing for faith and absolution. She treasured her connections with local priests, one of whom aborted a suicide attempt when she called him (the phone again!) seeking forgiveness before taking her own life. This ongoing ambivalence—wanting to die, wanting to stay alive—surfaces in the dream of the priest with a bad cold. Even as she pleads for death, Sexton turns her head to avoid catching it, as it were. I am aware of my own ironic stance in this fragment, and inside the irony my anger.

While I went on to write several other poems about our relationship, they are more direct, less revelatory, even, in one instance ("On Being Asked to Write a Poem in Memory of Anne Sexton") written in the third person. The final stanza of "Itinerary" contains what I think is the final dream I built on:

> Years pass, as they say in storybooks.
> It is true that I dream of you less.
> Still, when the phone rings in my sleep
> and I answer, a dream-cigarette in my hand,
> it is always the same. We are back at our posts,
> hanging around like boxers in
> our old flannel bathrobes. You haven't changed.
> I, on the other hand, am forced to grow older. . . .

The old relationship, grown bittersweet over the decades of her absence, recurs but now it contains a new element. Vivid, overt and unmysterious, these fragments cohere to remind me of our separate mortalities. Sexton remains static, forever forty-five. I am assigned to go on with my life:

> Now I am almost your mother's age.
> Imagine it! Did you think you could escape?
> Eventually I'll arrive in her
> abhorrent marabou negligee
> trailing her scarves like broken promises
> crying yoo-hoo! Anybody home?

Virtually every dream example I call up out of my poems teeters on the border between life and death. This seems quite apt to me, for I feel that poetry is essentially elegiac in its nature. We hold hard to those we love even as they die away from us and we continue to pursue them, through dreams into poems.

DENISE LEVERTOV

Schooled at home by her Welsh mother and Russian Jewish father, Denise Levertov grew up in England in an artistically fecund household. As a young woman she came to the United States where she became friends with William Carlos Williams, among others. Since then she published an avalanche of highly regarded poetry, including *The Jacob's Ladder* (1961), *Relearning the Alphabet* (1970), and more recently, *Evening Train* (1992) and *Sands of the Well* (1996). Always politically committed, Levertov's poetry has a strong meditative quality as well, as one sees in her recent books *The Life Around Us* and *The Stream and the Sapphire*, poems on nature and religion respectively. She died in 1997.

INTERWEAVINGS

Reflections on the Role of Dream
in the Making of Poems

an I distinguish between dreaming and writing—that is, between dream images and those which come into being while I am in the poem-making state? I'm not sure.

I began writing at a very early age, but the two childhood dreams I remember were beyond my powers to articulate. One of them was a kind of nightmare; and after it had recurred a couple of times I found I could summon it at will—which I did, in much the same spirit, I suppose, as that in which people watch horror movies. Retrospectively, I see it as a mythic vision of Eden and the Fall: the scene is a barn, wooden and pleasantly—not scarily—dark, in which the golden hay and straw are illumined by a glow as of candlelight. And all around the room of the barn are seated various animals—cows, sheep, horses, dogs, and cats. They all sit somewhat the way dogs do, with their front legs straight and their back ones curved to one side, and they look comfortable, relaxed. There's an atmosphere of great peace and well-being and camaraderie. But suddenly—without a minute's transition—all is changed: all blackens, crinkles, and corrugates like burnt paper. There is a sense of horror.

I was not more than six when I first dreamed this, and it frightens me still; can it (I think to myself) have been a prophetic dream about the nuclear holocaust we live in fear of? Then I console myself a bit with the knowledge that it didn't have to be so; I'd already long since been terrified several times by the sight of the newspaper my mother, with astounding rashness, would wrap around the metal-mesh fireguard to make the new-lit coals draw, catching on fire, the charred tatters of it flying up the chimney like flimsy bats. Someone had accidentally dropped a sheet of newspaper over my face when I was in the cradle and apparently I went into convulsions from the fright of it. I seem to remember it, in fact, though I was only a few months old; and this connected itself to the way a page of the *Times* would burst into a sheet of flame and so quickly blacken. In my dream there were no flames, only the switch from the soft glow in which all the friendly beasts (and I among them) basked and were at peace, to the horror of irreversible destruction, of ruin.

The other dream came when I was eight. I used as a child to love reading the descriptions (often accompanied by small photographs) of country houses for sale which at that time occupied the back page of the *London Times*. They ranged from cottages to castles, and I was not only fascinated by their varied architecture but also by their names. I would furnish each with inhabitants and make up "pretend games" (long, mainly unwritten serial stories within which I moved not so much *doing* anything as *being* one of the people in them—another form of dreaming). Another source of these daydreams was the sample notepaper, embossed or printed with the names of persons or places I presume were made up by the stationer, which my father, as a clergyman, used to receive from time to time. He would give me these advertisements to play with; and from a letterhead such as

> Colonel & Mrs. Ashley Fiennes
> The Manor House
> Rowanbeck
> Westmoreland

I could create not the *plot* of a story—I've never been good at that—but a situation and its shadowy children. So—this dream was of a house. When I first dreamed it there were some scenes, events, something of a story or situation in the dream; but those soon faded, and what I remembered (and now still either remember, or remember remembering, so that the picture still has clarity) was the vision of the house itself. It is seen from a hillside perhaps a quarter of a mile away, and it's a Jacobean house with two projecting wings. The stone it's made of is a most lovely warm peach-pink; and the English county it's in is Somerset—lovely name! The mood or atmosphere of this dream is as harmonious and delightful as that of the barn, but this time there's no disaster; it just goes on glowing, beaming, filling the self who gazes from the hillside with ineffable pleasure. Not long ago I realized that the reason I always give my present address as *West* Somerville, which though correct is not necessary for postal purposes, is not from some snobbish concern (East Somerville, like East Cambridge, is a poorer, uglier neighborhood) but because Somerville sounds like Somerset and Somerset is in the West Country. The associations are pleasant; when I say "West Somerville" I evoke for myself the old-rose color of the house in my dream, though plain "Somerville" makes me think of Union Square and its traffic jams. The house of the dream had a name too: Mazinger Hall; and I dreamed it on a Midsummer's Eve. For many years just to think of it could give me a sense of peace and satisfaction.

What connection do these two early dreams, which never became poems, have with the images of poetry or with my later activity as a writer? The powerful first one perhaps embodies some basic later themes, of joy and fear, joy and loss. But it's the second one—because of its verbal element, the house *having* a name and an awareness of the sounds and associations of *Somerset, West Country*, being implicit[1]—that links itself to the writing of poems.

Although my first book, *The Double Image*, is full of the words *dream* and *dreamer*, it is daydreaming and the *idea* of dreaming that really prevail in it. It was some years later that I began to write directly from real dreams; "The Girlhood of Jane Harrison,"[2] for instance. I had been

1. With connotations of *summer* and *sunset* included among them.
2. From *With Eyes at the Back of Our Heads* (1959) which, along with sections of *The Double Image* (1946), is included in *Collected Earlier Poems 1940-1960* (New York, New Directions, 1979).

reading J. H.'s *Prolegomena to the Study of Greek Religion* and some of her other work, but had not then read her charming autobiographical memoir, later given me by Adrienne Rich because I'd written the poem.

My dream is *described* in the poem, but I don't know that the sense, in the dream and in the wake of it, of the symbolic value of the window, indoor and garden darknesses, the sweetness of marzipan, the naming of roses, the diagram ("like the pan for starcake") of the dance in which Jane Harrison and her *semblances* moved from the central point out towards and beyond the dissolving boundaries of youth's garden, is adequately presented in the text. "Marzipan" is an especially unrealized reference; I myself can only dimly recall what part it played in the dream, and I don't see how anyone else could derive its significance from the poem unaided by any trace of memory. I think it was a word that the figure in the dream murmurs to herself as if its sound and the sweetness and dense texture of the substance so named expressed the feeling of the summer night and its roses. Also it was linked with the "star cake." The garden was a nineteenth-century English garden, with ample lawns and rosebeds, the surrounding shrubbery backed by taller trees, and a great cedar in the middle distance. Jane leans out of a ground-floor window at first; then she steps into the outdoor space. Though it's dark there's some moonlight, or possibly a glow from the house behind her—enough for trees and bushes to cast shadow. Starting from near the cedar, she begins to dance; and in forming the star figure of the dance, which is a ritual to welcome the autumn that is soon to begin, she multiplies, as if reflected in many mirrors or as if a cluster of identical dancers spread out to the points of a compass rose. She's moved out of the house of childhood, recognized the end of summer, saluted the fall (The Fall from innocence into the vast adventure of Knowledge?) to which her own grown-up life corresponds. Something like that. But as a poem it may be incompletely evolved, or partially unborn. And this is the great danger of dream poems: that they remain subjective, private, inaccessible without the author's gloss. Not only dream material presents this danger, of course; one of the most typical failures of student poetry is the writer's failure to recognize what has actually emerged into the poem and what remains available only to the poet or through explications not incorporated in the work. Such nonarticulated material may originate in all kinds of experience; but dream experiences are particularly likely to be insufficiently transmuted into art unless the writer is sensitive to the problem and to its solution.

"Relative Figures Reappear"[3] is another dream poem I seldom read to audiences. I feel it *describes* a dream but does not evoke it vividly enough for it to stir in others feelings analogous to those it gave to me; and because of this descriptive, rather than evocative, quality its *significances* remain unshared in much the same way as those in the Jane Harrison poem. "The Park" (also from the *Collected Earlier Poems*) on the other hand, in which persons and places of my own life also appear, seems somewhat more evocative—its images have more feeling-tone—and ends with a rather clear statement of intent, specifying the park as the

> country of open secrets where the elm
> shelters the construction of gods
> and true magic exceeds all design.

The dream (and I hope, the poem) gave a sense of the way in which "real magic" may be arrived at by means of illusive modes; or rather that it transcends the trickery or sleight-of-hand it may condescend to utilize. The elm (real, natural, an "open secret") may indeed shelter the construction, by carpenters, of wooden "gods"—but they are real gods! Magic is *happening*, a multilayered paradox.

Many of my poems of the fifties and early sixties—"Nice House," "Scenes from the Life of the Pepper Trees," "The Springtime," "The

---

3. *Collected Earlier Poems 1940–1960*

Departure" (all from the *Collected Earlier Poems*) for example—may seem to have been dream-derived, but they were not. Rather they are typical examples of the poetic imagination's way of throwing off analogues as it moves through, or plays over, the writer's life. I see a difference between these poems and those of a still earlier period, however: being more concrete and more genuinely related as analogies, metaphors, images, to that life experience (more rooted, in a word), they are truly poems in a degree that the stanzas of vague talk, unfounded either in actual dreams or in daily waking life, which filled *The Double Image*, were not.

One poem from the early 1960s which might easily be mistaken for dream account is "A Happening" (*Collected Earlier Poems*); here a metaphor that expressed for me the trauma of returning to the city after two years in Mexico, proved to be meaningful to many readers. For me it was New York City that was the intractably alien and terrifying place, despite years of residence there and attempts to love it; for others it may have been any other great metropolis. However, the poem includes a conscious irony that I now think is a flaw because of its peculiar obscurity: one of the protagonists (a stranger bird who turns into a paper sack and then "resumes its human shape" when it touches down in the streets of the city) goes uptown to seek the source of "the Broadway river." Now, only someone familiar with New York would know, first, that Broadway does have a riverlike meandering course, and second, that in fact it *begins* downtown, where Manhattan's earliest buildings were constructed near the harbor. So the stranger is looking in the wrong direction. That's part of the "plot" of the poem, but it's not fully accessible, and even to a New Yorker can too easily seem merely a mistake on the part of a writer who was, at the time, a fairly recent immigrant. (I had come to the United States at the end of 1949, but had spent almost four years out of the country during the fifties.)

In dreams, of course, just such "mistakes" do occur; but the dream *atmosphere* of a poem must be as strongly convincing as a Magritte painting to ensure the reader's not being distracted by its peculiarities from the dynamics of the poem itself. When the images of certain poems (dream derived or not) make one feel one is entering a real dream, it is a sign of their strength, their power. We are convinced—just as, ourselves dreaming, we accept without question situations and juxtapositions our waking reason finds illogical or "weird." Poems "about" dreams which are not well written are as boring or depressing as other shoddy work; and poems which (like my own early work) make constant reference to the dream state but provide no concrete evidence of its existence are at best vaguely pleasant in a melancholy, misty way. When a poem "feels like a dream" it does so by virtue of the *clearness* of its terms (however irrational they may be). When we wake from actual dreams, isn't it precisely the powerful clarity, not any so-called "dreaminess," that speaks to us? It is true that sometimes dream episodes, and figures in them, dissolve or melt into one another and that this witnessed metamorphic process forms part of the dream-drama; but we are not commonly brought to question it while dreaming, any more than we question the transitions of place, mood, and persons we experience while waking.

In the early sixties my husband began working with a Jungian therapist who encouraged him to talk over his dreams with me; and this stimulated me to remember and think about many more of my own dreams than hitherto, both because of our discussions and his account of the therapist's interpretations and because I began to make a practice of writing down what I remembered, and of participating to some extent in the emotional effect of Mitch's dreams as well as my own. Thus, in "A Ring of Changes" (*Collected Earlier Poems*), I wrote:

> I look among your papers
> for something that will give you to me
> until you come back;
> and find: "Where are my dreams?"

Your dreams! Have they not nourished my life?
Didn't I poach among them, as now on your desk?
My cheeks grown red and my hair curly
as I roasted your pheasants by my night fire!
    My dreams are gone off to hunt yours,
I won't take them back unless they find yours,
they must return torn by your forests . . .

It was a time of great pain and a lot of growth for us; looking back I see
that the sharing of our dream-life, and of what we were learning about
how to *think* about dreams, was what kept us going and held us to one
another in those years more than anything else. Whatever conflicts we
endured, we nevertheless found ourselves linked in the unconscious; not
that, as some have done, we dreamed the same dream or answered dream
with dream: yet our common intense interest in our own and each other's
nightly adventures in the inner world acted as a powerful bond. After a
while I too began to see a therapist and to work more methodically in trying to comprehend the symbolic language. Specifically dream-originated
poems of this time are part IV of "A Ring of Changes," "The Dog of Art,"
the prose story about Antonio and Sabrinus ("A Dream"), and "To the
Snake" (all from *Collected Earlier Poems*), as well as some of those previously mentioned: but not "The Goddess," though people have thought
so. The daisy-eyes, worked in wool, of "The Dog of Art" are the "lazy-
daisy" embroidered eyes my mother (and later I, myself, when my son was
little) used to substitute for the dangerous button eyes on wire pins with
which stuffed toy animals used to be furnished. The dream images, and
consequently the poem, imply relationships between the embroiderer's
practical creative imagination and the child's imagination, which infuses
still more life into the toy; the functioning of imagination in dream, and
the way it incorporates memory; and the way in which artists (of any
kind) draw upon all of these things. Daisies suggest the "innocent eye" of
art.

Something the Antonio and Sabrinus dream made even clearer for me than it had been before was the urgent tendency of some material toward its medium—in this case prose, not verse. I began telling the story as a poem, but it had been a dream with a very distinct tone or style, a *tale told*; and the slightly archaic diction which was virtually "given," or at least which the dream lay on the very brink of, sounded stilted in verse. (It was in conversation with Robert Bly that the possibility of capturing the tone better in prose rhythms emerged, I remember—unlikely as that seems, for Bly has never, in my opinion, really understood the sonic aspects of poetry, which is why, focusing almost exclusively on the image, he has felt free to translate such various poets. Had he been concerned with ear and voice he would have been daunted by auditory problems he has simply ignored.) The stanzas of verse which conclude "A Dream" began, I think, as the opening of the subsequently abandoned first version. I had a similar experience of material "wanting to be" prose in writing the nondream experience of a tree-felling, the story "Say the Word."[4] One must learn to listen to the form-needs of events; and dream material often seems to make this necessity specially clear.

This retrospective evaluation of my own relation, as a poet, to dreams reveals so far two main points. One is the difficulty of adequately conveying not only the mood of the dream, and not only describing or presenting its facts, but also—along with mood and facts combined—of capturing within the poem itself a sense of its significance. For the poem to work, this significance may be narrowly personal only if a sufficient context is provided for that personal meaning to justify itself as a dramatic component. For example, in "A Sequence"[5] it is possible (though I am not certain of it) that the tense situation presented in the first four parts of the sequence provides a sufficiently novelistic context for the

4. From *O Taste and See* (New York, New Directions, 1964).
5. From *The Jacob's Ladder* (New York, New Directions, 1961).

dream references of part five, tenuous though their meaning may be, to have some impact. One can at least comprehend that the dream joke (which, as often happens, doesn't really seem all that funny when one wakes and looks for the point of it) does in fact give a crucial moment of relief to the protagonists. And perhaps this puts it on a less narrow, more universal level: one accepts the laughter and relief (I speak now as a reader, not writer, for the poem was written so long ago) not because one shares the joke but because one has witnessed the characters' previous misery, and also because one is probably familiar with the way in which such tension can at last be broken by something simply silly.

The other point revealed is that the attempt to render dream into poem is potentially an excellent way to learn one's craft, for if the difficulties inherent in that process can be surmounted, those attendant upon the articulation of other experience seem less great. Moreover— and this perhaps is a third and separate point—consideration of dream images, in which the imagination has free play, or at least a play less censored, than it has in the waking mind, provides valuable models of possibility for the too-deliberate, cautious, and thus "uninspired" writer. (Or perhaps I should say, for the writer temporarily in an uninspired, overintentional phase; for if a poet's sole experience of being *taken over* by the imagination took place in dreaming, could one consider him a poet at all?)

There is a certain kind of dream in which it is not the visual and its associations which are paramount in impact and significance, but rather an actual verbal message, though a visual context and the identity of the speaker may be important factors. The first dream I can recall having written into a poem ("The Flight," *Collected Earlier Poems 1940-1960*), was dreamed in London in 1945 but not composed until several years later, probably in New York. The encounter with William Blake— who was sitting on the floor, his back against a wall and his knees drawn up, and whose prominent, unmistakable eyes gazed up at me as he spoke—was so memorable that the lapse of time has scarcely blurred it. And it coincided with the "real life" fact of a bird's getting caught in my room that night and at dawn, when I pushed down the top half of the sash window, shooting unhesitatingly out, calmed by the sleep into which it had sunk when I turned out the light. But it was the extraordinary Blakean words, "The will is given us that we may know the delights of surrender," that made the dream an artistic whole which seemed to ask only for transcription. Yet if I'd tried to write the poem at the time of dreaming I would not have had the craftsmanship to accomplish it, and it would have been lost to me, because once crystallized in an inadequate form it would almost inevitably have become inaccessible to another attempt.

Then there are verbal dreams whose visual context vanishes upon waking, or never appeared at all, the dream having consisted purely of words. The context may arrive later, in the world of external events. "In Memory of Boris Pasternak" (*The Jacob's Ladder*) exemplifies this latter eventuality. In its second section I wrote about the way in which a great writer can impart to scenes of one's own world a character they would not otherwise have had—in other words, can give one new or changed eyes to see through. It was while I was working on the poem, in a field in Maine, looking about me at the barn and woods and clouds, that I found and buried some dead fledglings among the wild strawberries; and as I was doing so, a dream I'd lost track of reentered my consciousness. When I had woken from it two nights before, I'd not associated it with the recently-dead poet; but now this verbal dream, a disembodied voice saying, "The artist must create himself or be born again," came clearly into the constellation of images and experiences clustered around my feeling for Pasternak; and the dictum seemed not only directive but also a comment on how, for the poet, "self-creation" consists in attaining, in a lifetime's practice of the art, the ability to reveal the world, or a world, to others. The dream words are syntactically ambiguous; do they mean,

"If the artist fails to give birth to himself (to his creative potential) he must undergo reincarnation until he does so"? Or is the syntax appositive, i.e., "The artist must create himself, or in other words be born anew in each work of his art, as in Christian theology the New Adam takes the place of the Old"? As the dreamer, my sense is that both meanings are implicit. Indeed, one of the most important lessons a poet can learn from dreaming is that, just as in dreams we effortlessly receive images and their often double significances, rather than force them into being by a process of will, so in writing (whether from dream or non-dream sources) the process is rather one of recognizing and absorbing the given than of willing something into existence. But this "given" is not the taken-for-granted reality of the superficial, inattentive, moving through life, but the often disregarded reality that lies just beyond or within it.

A dream that exemplifies the verbal message without visual or other sensuous context is this one, in which the following proposition was presented to the intellect (presumably in much the same way as solutions to mathematical problems have occurred to people during sleep):

"Trauerzucker = Zauberzucker"

The dream consisted of these equated possible German compounded words (which would mean "mourning sugar" and "magic sugar") and of the awareness (a) that (in the dream world) there exists a funeral rite in which lumps of sugar are distributed to guests at a wake, and (b) that this was understood to signify "out of sorrow comes joy." Thus, a ritual of sorrow and death, in which sugar is handed out to sweeten the bitterness, turns out to have an intimate connection with or even to be identical with (as shown by the equal sign) the rituals of (favorable, "white," or "good") magic—so that (it was implied) the sugar cubes don't just alleviate, but *transform* the sorrow (into joy).

A curious point was that the word trauer was misspelled, so to speak, in this nonvisual dream, as "trauber," a word that doesn't exist; however, the word "traube," meaning a bunch of grapes, does, so that *traubenzucker* would be "grape-sugar" (as in Trauben-saft, grape-juice).

Often a dream presents a ring from which to hang the latent questions of that moment in one's life. "The Broken Sandal"[6] was such a one. As it states, I "dreamed the thong of my sandal broke." The questions that follow—from the most literally practical ones about how I'm going to walk on without it over sharp dirty stones, to the more abstract ones

> Where was I going?
> Where was I going I can't go to now, unless hurting?
> Where am I standing, if I'm to stand still now?

—arise (gradually waking) from the initial event. The dream demanded of the dreamer that some basic life questions be asked. That was its function. In becoming poem, the organic process begun in dream continued, statement and questions giving the poem its necessarily terse form; and the mode of the questions was provided by the dream's sandal-thong metaphor, so that "Where am I (is my life) going?" is given concrete context, a matter of bare feet, of hobbling, of hurting. Finally the dreamer-writer is brought to enquire the nature of the place that is the poem's present. This type of dream-experience and poem-experience is not hampered by the intrusion of the ego and its so often untransferable trappings, but translates seamlessly into the reader's own "I". I wish this happened oftener. Yet perhaps a poetry devoid of the peculiarities of individual, even subjective experience might seem bland; occasionally such a poem may have some degree of stark force precisely because it is unusually simple, but a whole book of such poems might make one suspect the author of deliberately aiming at universality in the manner of gurus and greeting-card rhymesters. The hope is always that, when autobiographi-

6. From *Relearning the Alphabet* (New York, New Directions, 1970).

cal images occur in a poem, readers will respond with the same combination of empathy and of a recognition of their own equivalents with which they would receive a novel, a play, a film. For instance, in "Don't You Hear That Whistle Blowin . . . ,"[7] the "Middle Door" and the personages named—Steve, Richard, Bo, Mitch—are unknown to the reader, but the theme of the poem is loss and change, and my hope is that the poem clearly expresses this and (because of the givens of the dream source) reinforces that theme with the folkloric, nostalgic, associations of railroad trains.

There is a type of dream that, like the simple image of the broken sandal, virtually writes itself: the kind whose very terms are those of the myth or fairy tale. "The Well,"[8] about which I've written elsewhere, is an instance. More recently the nature of a close relationship was dreamed in what felt like mythic terms; the resulting poem ("A Pilgrim Dreaming"[9]) derived its rhythms and diction partly from the feeling-tone of the dream itself and partly from my waking feelings—rather awestruck—about having dreamed something seemingly from my friend's point of view rather than my own, almost as if I had dreamed his dream. Again, one of the two friends of whom I'd written twenty-five years before in "The Earthwoman and the Waterwoman"[10] (not a dream-derived poem) was visiting me one day in 1978, and after she left I dreamed about her as "The Dragonfly Mother,"[11] the long-ago images of water and blueness reappearing in a metamorphosis that expressed the growth and change in her and also in my response to her personality. Thus, the sequence was: impression, first poem, passage of time, new impressions, dream, second poem. And in addition (as recounted in the

7. From *The Freeing of the Dust* (New York, New Directions, 1975).
8. From *The Jacob's Ladder*.
9. From *Life in the Forest* (New York, New Directions, 1978).
10. From *Collected Earlier Poems*.
11. From *Wanderer's Day Song* (Copper Canyon Press. Port Townsend, Washington).

second poem) her visit affected my actions on that day, making me forego doing something I'd thought it was my duty to do (but which as a matter of fact wasn't important, since it was only a matter of speaking for two minutes at a big outdoor rally, at which I would not really be missed). Instead, I slept, dreamed, wrote a poem I like, and recognized how often the fear of displeasing masks itself as a sense of obligation.

Perhaps it is when dreaming and waking life thus interweave themselves *actively* that we experience both most intensely. When such interaction takes place for someone who is not able to incorporate it in any medium, the recognition of its power remains restricted to that individual. But the poet or other artist, as well as giving to dreams a corporeality that enables others to share them, may also sometimes experience the primary interweaving in the very doing of the poem, painting, dance, or whatever. It is then more than recapitulation, it is of one substance with the dream; and its power has a chance to extend beyond the limits of the artist's own life.

PHILIP LEVINE

Many of Philip Levine's poems come out of his experiences growing up in Detroit, where he attended public schools and later Wayne State University. He held a number of industrial jobs, often in automotive plants, before leaving Detroit for good. He studied poetry with Robert Lowell and John Berryman at the University of Iowa and eventually settled in Fresno, California, where he taught for many years. His collection *The Names of the Lost* won the Lenore Marshall Award in 1976. Since then more honors have accumulated: two National Book Awards, the Ruth Lilly Poetry Prize, and in 1995 the Pulitzer Prize for his volume *The Simple Truth*. Levine has also published essays, collected in *Don't Ask,* and a memoir, *The Bread of Time*. He currently teaches at New York University.

DREAM SONG

believe I'm fortunate in that I dream almost every night, and in my dreams I encounter an enormous cast of characters I otherwise would have no contact with: Hitler, Jackie Kennedy, Sonny Liston, Billie Holliday, Mr. and Mrs. Ronald Reagan. Occasionally in my dreams I create mythic figures who I feel should exist in the daily world, such as the Russian space explorer Cosmanaught P. Cosmanaught in whose company I made my first and only flight into space. In dreams I've accomplished things that have eluded me all my life. Although I am a great lover of jazz I have no gift for music nor any training as a performing musician, but one night—in sleep—I performed with the Sonny Rollins quartet. I sat before the drums at first dumbfounded until Sonny said, "Go ahead, Phil, it's easy," at which point I simply performed, and no one seemed to notice I had no idea what I was doing. In fact Sonny seemed perfectly delighted with my work. In dreams I find flying a small plane no more difficult than driving a car, but—alas—I always come back to earth at the same airport, the original Detroit airport on the city's east side. I've also spent time with dead friends, my fellow poets John Berryman, Jim Wright, and Larry Levis. In dreams I've allowed my two older sons to grow into manhood, as they've actually done, but my youngest, Teddy, remains Teddy at eight, with straight blond hair, incredible charm, and amazing articularity, the astonishing child he was. Curiously, my love life in dreams resembles my actual love life: I desire the same woman I'm actually sleeping beside, and I employ all sorts of ruses to get her clothes off when in truth she has no clothes on. Since I met her forty-four years ago never in sleep have I gone after another woman. This either suggests a profound lack of imagination or an unusually happy marriage. I should add that when I met her I thought her the most attractive woman I'd ever seen, and for me she remains that way.

In dreams I've written two poems and awakened remembering them word for word. This was forty-some years ago. I had quit working in Detroit and gone off with my small savings to study poetry writing at the University of Iowa with Robert Lowell, whose work I was in awe of. It was the first time in my life I could devote myself entirely to the writing of poetry. The fellowship that I expected to pay my tuition had been given to someone else. I could not afford out-of-state tuition and pay my room rent—$12 a month—and eat, so I simply lied and claimed I was registered, and neither Lowell nor John Berryman, who replaced him for the second semester, seemed to care. I was reading the work I loved eight hours a day, trying to write my own work, and working out in the university gym most afternoons. It was rather a monkish existence (until I met my wife-to-be), but I thrived on it. I relished the fact I was my own boss and that I was no longer helping produce objects that mysteriously made their way into the automobiles Detroit made, for as a production-line worker I rarely had the least idea what I was making. I was twenty-six years old, healthy, energetic, and with the aid of a few glasses of beer I rarely had trouble sleeping. Both Lowell and Berryman had urged me away from the poems of my beloved Hart Crane—"He leaves you no room to be yourself," John had said—and toward the work of Hardy and Frost. I found a used copy of the 1928 edition of Hardy's *Collected Poems* and worked my way painfully through its hundreds of poems. I found I had to read them all to find the gems, for some—like "Transformations"—I had never seen anthologized. I was so dazzled by several that without trying I memorized them while others with their clunky rhymes and antiquated diction seemed not to have been written by the same person. Thus one morning I awakened with a ballad in six rhyming stanzas in the voice of a young soldier about to go off to the Korean War, the war in which I had refused to serve, a poem I'd composed in a dream working at the very table that stood at the foot of my bed. In my blue flannel pajamas I rose from my narrow bed, sat on the room's only chair, and onto a yellow legal pad (the same sort of pad I'm writing on now), I penned the poem believing it to be a phenomenal gift. Did it sound like Hardy? Perhaps bad Hardy. As far as I know the poem no longer exists, but as best I can recall its diction was more Auden than Hardy, and it strived for some of that "spooky" quality that Auden got into his pre-WWII ballads and songs. The music was pure Hardy at his worst. I did not show it to Berryman, for in a curious way I felt it was not "me," was not in the voice I was beginning to locate or the voice that was beginning to locate me. I think it was probably better than almost anything I'd yet written.

When I completed the Hardy I turned to Shakespeare, *Measure for Measure* and *The Tempest*, both of which I read several times, but nothing came of this in my dreams. I even memorized certain passages in the hope they would serve as touchstones for the poems I hoped to write. In his modern poetry class Berryman announced we would be studying Stevens, and so I located a used copy of *Harmonium* and read and reread it with incredible delight. I'd always had great trouble penetrating his work, but for some reason he suddenly no longer seemed closed to me. I found the rhythmic mastery and richness of the diction breathtaking, and thus I began an internal conversation with Stevens that has never resolved itself. I wanted more of *my* world in his poetry, and he refused to give ground. Why should he? He was a great poet in his world, and he left me mine. Some years ago I read for his daughter Holly a poem that came out of this endless conversation, and she was delighted that a barbarian like me had taken "Dad" that seriously. The poem is called "An Ordinary Morning" but was originally "An Ordinary Morning Far from New Haven." The poem I wrote back there in 1954 in a dream was sixteen lines of blank verse, a meditation that owed everything to the master. Once again I awoke and copied the poem out, and once again I showed it to no one. I was glad I wrote it, for it seemed to demonstrate that I might write with his sort of elegance if I wanted to, a course I had no interest in following and actually no talent for. I wanted to depict my world.

None of what I've so far described is of much significance to my writing life, and if that were the only role dreams played in it I would not now be writing this piece. Ten years after composing my mediocre Hardy and my rotten Stevens I had a dream that changed the course of my writing life. I was living in Fresno, California, teaching good students at the state university there; the job was a hard one—four different courses each semester, mountains of papers to read and correct, the usual. I wrote mainly in the morning, rising before my sons did and working at the kitchen table, for I had no room of my own. One morning in April 1964 I wakened profoundly disturbed by a dream although nothing that terrible took place in the dream. It concerned a phone call I'd received from a man named Eugene Watkins with whom I'd worked in Detroit. What I remember most clearly about Eugene was that he had a finger missing, and I always feared working as his partner in schlepping for fear he could cause the same sort of accident that removed that finger. In the dream I could see Eugene calling from a phone booth beside U.S. 99 in Bakersfield, 120 miles south of where I lived. He'd called to tell me he was in California with his wife and daughter. He asked what they should do and see while they were in the West. I knew perfectly well that he was waiting for me to invite him to my home in Fresno, but instead I told him about the charms of L.A., Santa Barbara, Big Sur, San Francisco and about the fashionable restaurants and hotels neither he nor I could afford. Finally he thanked me and hung up. In the dream I saw him, head down, trudge to his car exactly as I would have in his place. Waking I was furious with myself for my lack of generosity, my snobbery. Why, I asked myself, had I betrayed him? Was it because he was black? I was living in a largely working-class neighborhood, black colleagues had visited me, black friends had stayed with us. Was I trying to escape my past? Did I think I was so hot with my assistant professorship at a second-rate college? What was I becoming?

It finally occurred to me that I had not betrayed Eugene or

rejected my past; I'd had a dream, and that dream was a warning of what might happen to me as a man and a poet if I turned my back on who I'd been and who I was. The kids were preparing for school so I climbed back into bed with my pen and legal pad. Almost immediately I was in that magical state in which poems simply come. I had my wife phone my department and say I was sick, and I stayed in bed for several days writing the first decent poems about my life as an industrial worker; all of them appeared in my second book, *Not This Pig*, published four years later; they are the core of the book and were the best poems I had then written. More important, they are the first poems I wrote that were not overwhelmed by the rage I felt toward the industrial life that had come close to devouring me; they are instead full of affection for the extraordinary people I'd met while living as a factory worker, the men and women who had done so much to teach me by their examples that life was a precious gift.

In 1953 I was working in a Detroit grease shop with a tall, slender black man with a wonderful wit and disposition. His name was Lemon Still Jr., and he was a delight to work with. One day we were dividing used crosses that are the heart of a universal joint, which is a component of a transmission and not an enormous reefer. One pile was junk, the other pile was made up of those which could be refinished and sold as new. Before we stuffed the hopeless ones into a burlap sack, Lemon held the bag before me and pointed at the white lettering which read, "Detroit Municipal Zoo," and he uttered a single memorable sentence, "They feed they lion they meal in they sacks." I was stunned by the sentence itself as well as Lemon's ability to simplify English grammar by reducing all third-person pronouns to the one "they." I don't know how many years passed before I forgot that moment, but in the late 1960s it came back to me via an unforgettable dream.

I dreamed I was hired by the boss of the same grease shop to serve as a night watchman. In the dream I said good night to the boss and to

Lemon and took up my duties to patrol a large fenced yard behind the shop in which the company's one truck was parked. Outside the fence in the dark were gangs of jeering teenagers, but none dared invade the property because I had as helpers not guard dogs but an enormous lion and an even larger elephant. The two animals walked ahead of me, and the teenage boys scattered in every direction, and then suddenly the elephant stopped and let go an enormous turd. And I awakened. And for some reason I remembered Lemon's astounding sentence. Some weeks later I attended a wedding party for a former student of mine, a lovely woman whose two brothers and mother had also been my students: I was the family poet and English teacher, and I was treated with great regard. After the wedding I danced—this was the late 1960s and everyone was encouraged to dance no matter how awkward he was. And so I danced, drank, and even had a few tokes of pot. I went home long after midnight feeling no pain, in fact feeling quite wonderful, for dancing outside in the Fresno heat I'd shed most of the toxins I'd taken into myself. I was tired and happy, and I fell into a profound sleep from which I awakened at six in the morning with the day just breaking outside my window. In my dream I had started to write a poem which began, "They Feed They Lion."

Before I could get any farther I'd awakened. I did not need to write it down; I knew I would not forget, and so I rolled over and went back to sleep. When I awakened that Sunday morning I did not sit down and try to write the poem. I felt I was still not ready, though I could feel it taking shape in my mind. I waited two more days during which I drank nothing alcoholic, exercised, and lived in moderation as the poem grew in me. On Tuesday morning I rose early and simply wrote it out, and except for one wrong move as I began the final stanza, which I quickly corrected by restarting the stanza, it came exactly as it still is for better or for worse.

They Feed They Lion

Out of burlap sacks, out of bearing butter,
Out of black bean and wet slate bread,
Out of the acids of rage, the candor of tar,
Out of creosote, gasoline, drive shafts, wooden dollies,
They Lion grow.
            Out of the gray hills
Of industrial barns, out of rain, out of bus ride,
West Virginia to Kiss My Ass, out of buried aunties,
Mothers hardening like pounded stumps, out of stumps,
Out of the bones' need to sharpen and the muscles' to stretch,
They Lion grow.
            Earth is eating trees, fence posts,
Gutted cars, earth is calling in her little ones,
"Come home, Come home!" From pig balls,
From the ferocity of pig driven to holiness,
From the furred ear and the full jowl come
The repose of the hung belly, from the purpose
They Lion grow.
            From the sweet glues of the trotters
Come the sweet kinks of the fist, from the full flower
Of the hams the thorax of caves,
From "Bow Down" come "Rise Up,"
Come they Lion from the reeds of shovels,
The grained arm that pulls the hands,
They Lion grow.
            From my five arms and all my hands,
From all my white sins forgiven, they feed,
From my car passing under the stars,
They Lion, from my children inherit,
From the oak turned to a wall, they Lion,
From they sack and they belly opened
And all that was hidden burning on the oil-stained earth
They feed they Lion and he comes.

Though the poem arrived after a joyous occasion, the wedding
party of someone I cared for, it is not a joyous poem, and though it was

written in a state of great calm it is far from peaceful. It is, I believe, the most potent expression of rage I have written, rage at my government for the two racial wars we were then fighting, one in the heart of our cities against our urban poor, the other in Asia against a people determined to decide their own fate. The poem was written one year after what in Detroit is still called "The Great Rebellion" although the press then and now titled it a race riot. I had recently revisited the city of my birth, and for the first time I saw myself in the now ruined neighborhoods of my growing up not as the rebel poet but as what I was, middle-aged, middle-class, and as one writer of the time would have put it "part of the problem." Out of a dream and out of the great storm of my emotions the poem was born.

GERARD MALANGA

© ASAKO

Gerard Malanga is a prolific poet, photographer, and filmmaker who first became known as an associate of Andy Warhol in the 1960s. Early works such as *Screen Tests/A Diary* and *chic death* show the influence of the Warhol ambience. But Malanga went on to publish more than a score of other books, including *Mythologies of the Heart* (1996), which leave the Factory days far behind. An accomplished photographer, his work has been collected in two monographs: *Good Girls* and *Resistance to Memory*. He presently lives and works in New York City.

THE STUFF THAT DREAMS ARE MADE OF

There are many approaches and volumes of books on what dreams are made of. Freud wrote extensively on dreams, as did Jung. Yet other reflections are equally fascinating.

Jack Kerouac, in the Foreword to his collection, *Book of Dreams* (City Lights, 1961), describes the process in which he retrieved dreams from his sleep: "They were all written spontaneously, non-stop, just like dreams happen, sometimes written before I was even wide awake." *Just like dreams happen* is very much the method my own dream dictation takes shape.

One thing's for certain—what occurs in the dream is the elimination of rational thought and memory that might interfere with how the unconscious functions as a liberating force; for we are never more free than in our dreams.

But how does all this relate to poetry? Coleridge once remarked that poetry is the willing suspension of disbelief. Dream, in essence, is the mirror of this suspension—the reverse side of conscious reality.

The mirror is a metaphor for what is ephemeral, irretrievable. Yet it allows us to be observers of ourselves. We see ourselves flying through space or moving at great speeds, talking with ex-girlfriends, encountering the dead.

Often what seems most obscure in the dream is what finally reveals a deeper meaning through poetry. Images, ideas, actions and the like, are key elements that make up the dream; even disembodied voices/felt presences. The way we connect these elements provides the basis for how the dream poem evolves: How much of what we dream we can wake with to make the poem happen.

André Breton, the founder of Surrealism, knew how dreams could be turned into poems. His book essay, *The Communicating Vessels*

(Les Vases Communicants), published in 1932, is not only one of the great surrealist works; it is also the most important work on dreams since the publication of Freud's *Interpretation of Dreams* in 1899. Don't take my word for it. Read on, or better yet, here's a hint:

> Every means should continue to be tested to see more clearly, while separating it from the irrational certitude accompanying it, what can be taken for true or false. It is worthwhile not only that we refuse to abandon any of the proved modes of intuitive knowledge, but also that we work towards new ones. Once again, nothing can be more necessary in this respect than a profound examination of the process of the formation of images in sleep, aided with what can be learned, on the other hand, from poetic elaboration. How is it that some such images are retained in preference to others, among all others?

The question of how one goes about turning one's dreams into poetry will find no answer from me this morning. Most dreams are never remembered. We dream in order to forget.

Gone fishin'.

Morning of January 2, 1993

Why would Danny Campana speak to me
through early morning dream forty years later
as intimate friend?
His words heard not as words,
But as needing help.

He would have to be nearly my mom's age now—87.
Maybe a bit older even . . . I don't know.
It was to have been my last summer
vacation in the Catskills I recall,

and now being delivery boy
for Danny's Fruit & Vegetable Produce—
slope of East 194th Street, the Bronx—
would last well into the 7th grade,
Creston Junior High.

To me I was just a kid in his eyes,
simply in his employ, like they say,
defined by a chance at proving myself
and earning my way for the first time.
I could ride a bike. Beyond that,
nothing defined us as close.

Rugged, good looks, charming, sweep of black hair
turning grey at the edges—a lit cigarette, a CAMEL,
dangled from his lips whenever I'd see him
lift bushels of produce
in and out of the store,
ring up the register,
take a breather, now and then, out back
where I'd hang out too,
between orders.

My mom was a regular customer.
They got on well.
She had good credit.

Where is Danny Campana
who touched me this morning with his soul . . .

whose spirit visits me now?

Where is he now?

What is the message he brings
for me to decipher?

Why me?

What is he to be remembered for?

What is this thing called dream?

PAUL MARIANI

Paul Mariani, poet, biographer, and critic, is Distinguished University Professor at the University of Massachusetts, Amherst, where he has taught since 1968. He is the author of five books of poetry, including *Salvage Operations: New and Selected Poems* (1990) and *The Great Wheel* (1996), and has written major biographies of William Carlos Williams, Robert Lowell, and John Berryman. His most recent biography is *Hart Crane: Making New York* (Norton, 1998). For many years Mariani taught at the Bread Loaf

Writers' Conference and later served as dean of the Glen Eyrie Writers' Workshop in Colorado Springs. His awards include two National Endowment for the Humanities fellowships, an NEA for poetry, a Guggenheim, and the New Jersey Writers' Award for his work on William Carlos Williams.

DREAM SCRIPTS

Tempest-tossed Prospero, magician, poet, creator, in the act of drowning his book, waking now from the ether of his long dream into the light of day, saying:

> The charm dissolves apace;
> And as the morning steals upon the night,
> Melting the darkness, so their rising senses
> Begin to chase the ignorant fumes that mantle
> Their clearer reason. . . .

Or Richard Gere, speaking with Oprah Winfrey, on a late afternoon, October 1997, on the subject of Buddhist meditation. That at its best it seems to clear the air of low-lying clouds so that the mind may stare upon the stars. With regard to dreams and poems: my sentiments exactly. The dawn hour, when at last we wake from the dream of our lives.

After all, it is a dream, isn't it? At least our language says it's so. Take the beginning of the Bible, with its dream of creation and of our ghostly origins. Take the nightmare scenarios of the ancient myths, take Gilgamesh, Oedipus's dream of killing his father, of sleeping with his mother. Take the Middle Age's enormously influential *Dream of Scipio*. Take Freud, or the Everley Brothers singing, "Dream, dream, dream . . . ," or Joyce's twenty-year dream of *Finnegans Wake*, or Williams's old dream of *Paterson*, or Rip, or Hart Crane waking to a white fog drowning New York Harbor and the East River, or Berryman's *Dream Songs*, Lowell's dream of *History*, Martin Luther King's "I have a dream."

Who hasn't a poem that owes something to dreams, acknowledged or not? I look back at my own poems now, and see how many of them are transcripts of dreams or dreamlike states. Rivers, foggy-bottom reveries. How often poems I once wrote seem to say something other than what I took them to say, as if the words themselves were dreams which had assumed a life of their own, and were about to turn on their circus master as he awakens now to find a whip in his hand and teeth gnashing at him. How many of these same poems seemed so benign once, therapeutic exorcisms, which now—like some final judgment—come back snarling, straining against their chains. To think my own poems might have blood on them. And yet, all five poets I have written of—Hopkins, Williams, Berryman, Lowell, Hart Crane—have told us it was darker inside than they (or we) had ever imagined.

Let me try to put some order around what it is I'm saying. There are a dozen poems I can point to which came directly out of dreams, dreams so vivid I had to get them down on paper. Several were nightmares, from which I woke in a sweat. A few were more consoling, or became so in the blessèd break of dawn, as if a fever had finally broken. Strangely, even as I write these words, the words themselves seem dreamlike as I watch these old poems, not read for years, begin to reconfigure themselves like old man Proteus.

Waking daydreams. Isn't that what Father Freud tells us poems are, the twilight zone where writing seems less like writing and more like transcription, words awakening with marching orders of their own, urging us to write this and this and this? It doesn't matter that you understand what it is that is being dictated. Sometimes, in fact, the best writing comes out of merely following the words themselves. It is as if up to that point you were doing warm-up exercises, five-finger things, then suddenly began composing serenades.

The barriers break down, the dog that bounded about behind the fence suddenly jumps the fence, off after a scent. You write. The words flow, the current leaps or eddies, runs smooth or jostles, as word gives way to word. Or the words lodge and jam. Later that day or the next or a week or a year or years later—what matter, it's all dreamtime anyway, isn't it?—you go back to the lines again, to find something that vitally concerns you, something of profound interest. A matter, perhaps, of life and death.

Say, for instance, that you're married and you've raised a family. Say you think you've been a good father, a decent father who, in spite of the inevitable shortcomings that come with being a human animal, has managed to raise sons and do a passable job of it. The best schools and all the rest. Say you spend an hour, going back to examine the partial record of your kids, a record you kept in your poems of their various goings and comings, and of your comings and goings with them. Then, say, a bearded prophet—woman or a man, what matter?—walks in, sits down, lights up a cigar, and asks you to explain such and such an image. The bud of sex, say, and here's a razor, and here's a father and a son going up a mountain, and here's an altar and a fire. And because you are no longer the same person you were when you wrote the poem, you note the images have changed their protective coloration.

Here's an example: lines I wrote twenty years ago, from a poem in unrhymed quatrains called "What the Wind Said." The father—that's me in the picture—is in Buffalo, doing research. Back home—that would be a small town situated north of Amherst—three sons and a wife. The father, alone there in a hotel room in Buffalo, thinks, remembers, dreams. Because he's a professor, he thinks in literary analogs (Greek myth, *Henry IV*, Genesis, Luke's Gospel, and so on), thinking in that way to universalize what is—when all is said and done—a painful personal experience.

As dreams also do, insulating us from the horror. After all, when all's said and done, hell's a fine and private place, isn't it?

> Four hundred airborne miles. That's
>
> rope enough to let my words wind out.
> Frailest cable. Ariadne's thread.
> Trundling your Buddha-bellied flailing
> body corded up in cotton blanket
>
> like some half-inflated basketball,
> the unconscious sacrifice of Isaac,
> rammed wedgelike through the unrelenting
> winter of my own youthful discontent.
>
> My own Prince Hal, half rebel son,
> half intent on pleasing. That cocksure,
> uneasy strut of yours, as if the world
> was yours. And yet you had to hide
>
> your head before you could bring yourself
> to talk of "it." Your budding sense
> of sexuality. Crocus nudging through
> last year's harvest of dead leaves
>
> and fretty snow, a growing, as the saying
> goes, in age and grace and wisdom.
> How the spring stem holds against
> the searing ceaseless winds. How the young
>
> grass repairs itself again. . . .

Let's see. What else do I remember of the poem now? U. of Buffalo, late winter, 1980. I've come here to immerse myself in the extensive Williams collection for the biography of the poet I am writing. The life of the life of the poet. Three sons—14, 12, 11—at school in western Massachusetts. I've just turned forty, a professor of English at U. Mass, a commentary on Hopkins out, another on Williams, a book of poems. I miss my family, but I've chosen to come here at the family's expense to get this new book done. There are better places I can think of being than Buffalo in March, or Buffalo at any time for that matter, but that is where the stuff I need is found.

I remember walking across campus, seeing gray snow mounds where the huge plows had piled winter's detritus. A freezing rain had fallen, making even walking treacherous, and now a strong wind is blowing. It is so cold the metal rims of my glasses burn against my cheeks, the ridge of my nose. The terrazzo tiles on which I walk seem to break or do break under my feet, from water which has seeped under them and frozen. Some insane architect's dream conceived in summer, breaking up in winter as the returning sun warms the pavement. Like a bad dream, one might say, this solid exterior crackling beneath.

A telephone call, an umbilical cord, Joyce's Adam to any of us down the line, linked line to line (Omphalos-1234, Operator). The poem too linked word to word, line to line. Cordage as communication, cordage as binding, sacrifice. Carrying my infant son like a football, a young father disbelieving this bundle he had just returned from christening in church was real, and his. A dream, carrying his boy like a football, bumping the baby's head against the car door, the little hands flailing open and shut.

The son's need to have his own space, the father wanting to protect, or the father setting too strict guidelines—as in the poem, four beats for five, perhaps? The father anxious for his son, wanting him to win through in every way. (He must increase. I must decrease.) Who knows why we do the things we do? But there it is, in the record of those lines. A truth bigger than the one I thought I brought to the poem. Dreams do that, though, don't they? The way myths do, carrying the seeds of the whole story in each poem.

Here's another poem, one that goes back to the summer of 1991. Same father, same son, both older. Now it's the son who's left, having traveled halfway round the world to Taiwan, there to study Chinese, having now to undergo an operation in the hospital there. He's called collect, given us the news, and won't or can't hang up. The father—that's me—finally turns the phone over to his wife and begins to calculate what the call will cost collect, putting those other costs on hold, costs that likewise leave their mark upon the soul. Quatrains again, clipped:

> When my oldest boy calls home (collect)
> via satellite, his small voice
> sounds as if he were just around the corner
> instead of halfway round the world.

> He tells us, yes, he will have to have
> the operation there in Taiwan: general
> anesthetic & a week-long stay in semi-
> private quarters, & keeps playing

> the same facts over, unwilling
> to hang up, while I watch my phone bill
> yanked screaming into orbit.
> I am all abrupt advice, while my wife,

> on the phone inside, remains solicitude itself,
> so that, hanging up, I know
> I've screwed it up again, having learned
> nothing of what it costs to play the father. . . .

First half of poem. A man trying to play the father. Communication established, then cut off. Which brings to mind an old dream of unselfworth and abandonment, between the speaker and *his* father. And so it's back to the drawing board again, dredging up the muck of an old dream, an old movie, black and white, grainy, such as Delmore saw—strobe-lit, fitful—to try to make some sense out of what I've done and why I've done it:

> And so I will have to go back down
> another time to see what I can see,
> dredging up once more the ill-lit nightmare
> which stars my father and myself.

Trapped behind the wheel again,
I will watch with horror the ancient Plymouth
sink into the black canal. Once again
I will try to kick the window out

while I wrestle for a mouth of air,
cold water rising swiftly to the roof,
until everything goes numb. And once the winch
has finally dragged us up, I watch

my father watching. He slides a hand
across the chilly hood, then lets it ride
the green teeth of the broken window.
He knows there's nothing left inside

for him to work with anymore. But once
the window's fixed and the upholstery dried
and cleaned, he figures he could still
get something for the Plymouth.

It's an old dream, this one, and has crept its way into more poems of mine than I care to remember. There's an incident that happened up in Turners Falls, six miles north of here, on an old canal that sluices off the Connecticut River to supply power to an electric substation at the far end of the canal. A car somehow disengaged, rolled back, crashed through the flimsy guard rail and sank to the bottom of the canal, drowning the two children inside before anyone could get to them. That car sank as well into the detritus and muck of my own unconscious and lodged there, to resurface in my nightmare.

Growing up, we had an old Plymouth. My father, being a mechanic, brought home many used cars, but the Plymouth I see chimes with that other Plymouth: a covenant in a new land, the nascent American dream, Indian scalps and all. A variation, all in all, this dream, of men sending their sons off to war to preserve a way of life in the name of liberty or freedom or truth or some other too easy abstract. Abraham and Isaac again. After all, you don't live through the hundred years' war called Vietnam—combatant or no—without someone paying, right, Lyndon? Right, Paul?

Let's try it one more time. Another family drama, this time starring yours truly and his own brothers and sisters (six—count them). The poem is "Ghost." It's a waking dream, so vivid I swear it must have had its origins in a nightmare sometime back. Many times, in fact. It's an Easter Sunday, five or six years back. Eileen and I have invited as much of my scattered family as can make it. I'm washing the dishes in the kitchen, talking with my brother Patrick, who is out of work again—let go because the company he'd been working for was about to go under because of bad debts.

He's eleven years my junior, but bigger, stronger, more vulnerable. I'm listening, but his troubles are beginning to drain me, and there's little I can do about the situation. ("Shit. You're out of work? That's too bad. Have a nice day." You know the routine.) And as with "Salvage Operations," it hits me all at once: the guilty dream, the pain of abandonment, my impatience to break free and away from this. Here's the poem:

> After so much time you think
> you'd have it netted
> in the mesh of language. But again
> it reconfigures, slick as Proteus.
>
> You're in the kitchen talking
> with your ex-Navy brother, his two kids
> snaking over his tattooed arms, as he goes on
> & on about being out of work again.
>
> For an hour now you've listened,
> his face growing dimmer in the lamplight
> as you keep glancing at your watch
> until it's there again: the ghost rising
>
> as it did that first time when you,
> the oldest, left home to marry.

You're in the boat again, alone, and staring
at the six of them, your sisters

& your brothers, their faces bobbing
in the water, as their fingers grapple
for the gunwales. The ship is going down,
your mother with it. One oar's locked

and feathered, and one oar's lost,
there's a slop of gurry pooling
in the bottom, and your tiny boat
keeps drifting further from them.

Between each bitter wave you can count
their upturned faces—white roses
scattered on a mash of sea, eyes fixed
to see what you will do. And you?

You their old protector, you their guardian
and go-between? *Each man for himself,*
you remember thinking, their faces
growing dimmer with each oarstroke.

What's netted in the language? Meaning? Distance? Order? A
buffer of some sort? A primal cry turned palatable by playing the stops
until some song is sculpted from the pain? But something does get
dredged up from the underworld of dream, doesn't it? In yet another form,
like sea-changing Proteus, master of disguises. And there's your brother,
like Laocoön and his two sons in Virgil's telling (which I ponied as a
young man in Latin IV), about to be destroyed by those serpents slither-
ing up the shore to kill them all for bearing witness to the terrifying truth:

At first each snake entwines the tiny bodies
of his two sons in an embrace, then feasts
its fangs on their defenceless limbs. The pair
next seize upon Laocoön himself. . . .

You've heard it all before, and now you're tired. You've made it. He has-n't. Others haven't. The snakes aren't after you, anyway. Fuck, who needs this? It's Easter.

And then the dream. A lifeboat, your parents in the long agony of their marriage and ultimate divorce finally going under. Alcohol ("white roses / scattered on a mash of sea," a whiskey mash) superimposed upon the appalled, blanched faces of my siblings, caught in the undertow (or is it undertoad?) as the ship—like some *Titanic*—goes down, like the Plymouth in the last poem, its detritus to resurface later. And though you know you've always tried to be there for them, you fear you really have abandoned them, as your brother Walter has often tweaked you for. Right?

It's an old story, really, this domestic tragedy which you fear will go on replaying itself in your own life in spite of all you do to plug the holes. After all, you're really a good guy (right?), smiling on all who smile upon you. You have more money than your parents ever did, and you're a professional. What a good boy am you. Except that there are these god-dam dreams that keep coming back at you. And the poems you wrote in the hope of exorcising some old demons, but which—being poems—have come back to haunt you, setting the record straighter than you ever thought. Is that what the Last Judgment will taste like, as Father Hopkins says, a place where "thoughts against thoughts ín groans grind"?

Not a happy thought, this, eh, friend? But true enough. Something of yourself in what's been said here? *Mon semblable, mon frère?* The taste is bitter but it doth bring health. Well, there are other dream scripts in this book to look upon. Here. Lend me your hand to turn the page for you.

J. D. McCLATCHY

J. D. McClatchy has published four volumes of poetry: *Scenes from Another Life* (1981), *Stars Principal* (1986), *The Rest of the Way* (1990), and *Ten Commandments* (1998). He has also authored two collections of essays, *White Paper: On Contemporary American Poetry* (1989) and *Twenty Questions* (1998), and edited several other books. The versatile author has moonlighted as a librettist, collaborating with four composers; and most recently, his opera *Emmeline*, with music by Tobias Picker, was revived by the New York City Opera at Lincoln Center. He is the editor of the *Yale Review* and a chancellor of the Academy of American poets.

SOME FOOTNOTES TO MY DREAMS

I n his *Life of Shelley*, Jefferson Hogg relates a story he once heard about Wordsworth. The poet used to keep pencil and paper by his bedside, and when a thought occurred to him in the night, or he awaked suddenly from a dream, he would write it down instantly, without lighting a candle. Through long habit he was able to write in the dark. When Shelley heard about it, he experimented with his method of retrieving the fading embers of the unconscious. But, it is reported, he usually dropped his pencil, or his paper, or both; and when he managed to hold on to both, in the morning he found the writing was illegible.

I rarely remember my dreams, but when I do they seem to have involved a pretty straightforward—that is, easily decoded—processing of the previous day's agenda of thwarted desires and overdrawn anxieties. There are a few recurring dreams, however. They are invariably a puzzle to be solved: a vaguely familiar situation into which I am put or have wandered, and which I must escape or master. Just last night, for instance, there was a variant of the most common. I am back in college. It is toward the end of a semester, and I suddenly realize that I haven't been attending an English course I'd signed up for. (It's as likely to be a course in physics or Urdu, but last night it was English.) Exams are approaching and I haven't any idea what I should have been studying—though I've skipped classes, in part, because I am haughtily convinced I know it all. I find the room, and take my seat (last night, I was sitting by chance next to George Plimpton). The teacher is an attractive young black woman. She's explaining a point of grammar, and to illustrate it has positioned several pieces of toast on a shelf attached to the blackboard. Oh, but her point is so obvious, and the others in class seem confused. It has to do with the use of the word "rather" in a sentence. It's clear to me, as to no one else, that the third slice of toast is out of place. . . . Well, this is all too obvious. My eventual shame and further confusion in that classroom I shall leave to your imagination.

The toast reminds me, though, of another matter. Almost the first thing I do every morning after getting up is the *New York Times* crossword puzzle—in pen and rather quickly. I do it as obsessively as I dream certain dreams. It's not the difficulty of the crossword that attracts me, but the reassurance that *here*, in *this* puzzle, for every question there is an answer, and for every answer there is a question.

If we move these two terms to the realm of poetry, is a poem more like a *dream* or a *puzzle*? When a reader first encounters a strong poem, it is likely to strike him as a dream—a text replete with meaning that is mysteriously both proffered and withdrawn. Correspondingly, when the idea—or better to say, instinct—for that poem first glimmered in the poet's own mind, and as he begins to work it up on paper, the poem is also likely to resemble an unfolding dream. Only later, when the poet is revising a final draft, or the reader has understood its depths and implications, will the poem seem to each a puzzle, intricately constructed and apparently solved. But truly great poems—think of a hymn by Emily Dickinson or an ode by Elizabeth Bishop—are puzzles that remain dreams.

Let this memory of mine give an example. I was in school, toward the end of the semester. This time—awake and never missing a class—I was in graduate school. My teacher was Cleanth Brooks, one of the most learned and subtle readers of poems, and a man whose method had taught several generations of readers how to approach a poem. He and I were walking down the street one afternoon in New Haven, and Mr. Brooks was musing out loud. We were discussing Wordsworth. "You know," he said, "the older I get, and the more I read Wordsworth, the less I understand him." He was not, of course, underestimating either's powers; rather, he was acknowledging a fact about all great poets—that the terms of their poetic selfhood, the sublime leaps their poems make, will forsake us if we presume to think we have comprehended them.

With the years, it gets so that what I remember is having had an experience, but I can no longer exactly recall the experience itself. There is a snapshot, not a movie. For instance, I remember that, about thirty years ago, I had a series of vivid dreams about Ben Jonson. He looked rather like the familiar contemporary portrait of him now in the National Portrait Gallery in London: but studious and swaggering, bully and bard. I remember that in my dream he was dressed more raffishly than in his portrait; that we were in a pub; that I was shy and content to listen as he held forth on all manner of topics. But what he said—pretty clear three decades ago, and interesting enough for me to resume the sessions several nights in a row—is lost to me now.

But the other time I dreamt about a writer remains both clear and haunting. I got to know Anne Sexton around 1972. We grew to be friends, and were an odd pair. She was by then a celebrity, and a wreck. But a glamorous and compelling one—constantly looped on vodka and pills, desperately divorced, mentally unstable, but dressed in a long red satin dress with her husky voice and raucous laugh. I, on the other hand, was a serious-minded graduate student, nervously gay, wide-eyed. When I first visited her, to do an interview, I arrived at her suburban house on the dot of eleven, as agreed. One of her daughters answered the door, explained that her mother wasn't feeling well and was still in bed, and would I wait in the living room please. An hour passed. The daughter reappeared and asked if I'd follow her upstairs. Mother was still in bed, but would see me there. I was shown into the bedroom. Anne was in the midst of a huge bed, propped up on pillows, in a swank bathrobe. She motioned me to a chair. I mumbled something about not wanting to trouble her. That launched her on an account of her recent woes and illnesses. She wound up with the latest complaint, rubbing her hands over her robe. "And I have very sensitive nipples," she said. "You'll see."

Yikes. I'd only just been introduced. Oh, but all that sorted itself out soon enough, and we became pals. Within a couple of years, she asked if I would serve as her literary executor (I declined)—a request, I only realized later, that was part of a determined and gradual withdrawal that culminated in her suicide. A couple of weeks before she killed herself, she was calling me from the pay phone in a mental hospital, insisting she was receiving radio transmissions in her cavities and would I come check her out of this hellhole. My sympathy pulsed, but even I knew enough not to intervene. She came home. I called in. And when, one day that I telephoned, I was told by a housekeeper that Anne was in Baltimore, giving a poetry reading, and would return tomorrow, I said that I'd call back the day after. In fact, I forgot to do so. That night, I had a dream. I was watching the evening news. Walter Cronkite was announcing that the Pulitzer Prize–winning poet Anne Sexton had died, and behind him was an inset showing some sort of grainy home movie of her. She was sitting on a sofa, with a child on her lap. She had on a dress and a hair-do that resembled photographs of my mother when I was small. And the child in her lap, I then noticed, was a young boy, in shorts and a horizontally striped T-shirt, with a buzz cut. I recognized him as well. Sexton had no son. The boy was myself. Early the next morning, the dream throbbed—when, suddenly, the phone rang. It was Howard Moss. He wondered if I'd heard the news. Yesterday, Anne Sexton had committed suicide.

My dream, of course, had to do with my guilt at not having telephoned her when I'd promised to. But the coincidence was more than uncanny and remains as my only (unreal) experience of precognition. I could as easily—as I do now—have read her last poems to see the same unwinding, the same cries and whispers, the same stark refusals. As a reader, instead of as a dreamer, I could have been a child on her lap.

It is no wonder we pay people to listen to our dreams. As an apt analogy, Leopardi suggested would-be poets should underwrite an audience for their poems: hired listeners in a small amphitheater, the size of a steam room, paid to listen, murmur, applaud.

Novalis: "Is sleep a mating with oneself?" Dreams and poems resemble each other in nothing so much as their autoeroticism.

Nothing, after all, is so logical as a dream. All the connections are there, but disguised or concealed. That is why it is not surrealist gibberish that is most dreamlike. Nor even those exquisite epiphanic poems by James Wright that are the best of the "deep image" wing. Oh, there are extraordinary waking dreams that muse over the collective unconscious, like James Merrill's *The Changing Light at Sandover*. But for my money, the most dreamlike poem I know, because it elaborates a private knowledge into a grand myth, is John Hollander's *Reflections on Espionage*. The whole relationship between a master spy and his control is an uncanny trope on the business of dream work.

But there is a way too that many strong poems resemble dreams—or perhaps I should say sleep. If we consider the four stages of sleep, each with its distinctive characteristics—light sleep, followed by "spindles" and rolling of eyes, followed by deep sleep with its slower brain waves and lowered heart rate, followed by the deepest sleep of all, out of which the sleeper emerges into the REM state—could we follow a similar pattern in certain poems? We are familiar enough now with the dynamics of REM, that "internal storm" of nearly hallucinatory sensations on which both our psyches and our bodies depend. And now, when I read "Tintern Abbey" or "Ode to a Nightingale" or "The Auroras of Autumn," *The Bridge* or *The Waste Land*, what I sense is this same movement inward, a deeper concentration, then a release of fearsome energies.

Three Dreams About Elizabeth Bishop

I.
It turned out the funeral had been delayed a year.
The casket now stood in the State Capitol rotunda,
An open casket. You lay there like Lenin
Under glass, powdered, in powder blue

But crestfallen, if that's the word
For those sagging muscles that make the dead
Look grumpy. The room smelled of gardenias.
Or no, I *was* a gardenia, part of a wreath
Sent by the Radcliffe Institute and right behind
You, with a view down the line of mourners.
When Lloyd and Frank arrived, both of them
Weeping and reciting—was it "Thanatopsis"? —
A line from Frank about being the brother
To a sluggish clod was enough to wake you up.
One eye, then the other, slowly opened.
You didn't say anything, didn't have to.
You just blinked, or I did, and in another room
A group of us sat around your coffin chatting.
Once in a while you would add a comment—
That, no, hay was stacked with beaverslides,
And, yes, it was a blue, a mimeograph blue
Powder the Indians used, and stuck cedar pegs
Through their breasts in the ghost dance—
All this very slowly. Such an effort for you
To speak, as if underwater and each bubble-
Syllable had to be exhaled, leisurely
Floated up to the surface of our patience.
Still alive, days later, still laid out
In a party dress prinked with sun sparks,
Hands folded demurely across your stomach,
You lay on the back lawn, uncoffined,
Surrounded by beds of freckled foxglove
And fool-the-eye lilies that only last a day.
By then Lowell had arrived, young again
But shaggy even in his seersucker and tie.
He lay down alongside you to talk.
The pleasure of it showed in your eyes,
Widening, then fluttering with the gossip,
Though, of course, you still didn't move at all,
Just your lips, and Lowell would lean in
To listen, his ear right next to your mouth,
Then look up smiling and roll over to tell me
What you said, that since you'd passed over

You'd heard why women live longer than men—
Because they wear big diamond rings.

II.

She is sitting three pews ahead of me
At the Methodist Church on Wilshire Boulevard.
I can make out one maple leaf earring
Through the upswept fog bank of her hair
—Suddenly snapped back, to stay awake.
A minister is lamenting the forgetfulness
Of the laws, and warms to his fable
About the wild oryx "which the Egyptians
Say stands full against the Dog Star
When it rises, looks wistfully upon it,
And testifies after a sort by sneezing,
A kind of worship but a miserable knowledge."
He is wearing, now I look, the other earring,
Which catches a bluish light from the window
Behind him, palm trees bent in stained glass
Over a manger scene. The Joseph sports
A three-piece suit, fedora in hand.
Mary, in a leather jacket, is kneeling.
The gnarled lead joinder soldered behind
Gives her a bun, protruding from which
Two shafts of a halo look like chopsticks.
Intent on her task, her mouth full of pins,
She seems to be taking them out, one by one,
To fasten or fit with stars the night sky
Over the child's crib, which itself resembles
A Studebaker my parents owned after the war,
The model called an Oryx which once took
The three of us on the flight into California.
I remember, leaving town one Sunday morning,
We passed a dwarfish, gray-haired woman
Sitting crosslegged on an iron porch chair
In red slacks and a white sleeveless blouse,
A cigarette in her hand but in a silver holder,
Watching us leave, angel or executioner,
Not caring which, pursuing her own thoughts.

III.
Dawn through a slider to the redwood deck.
Two mugs on the rail with a trace
Still of last night's vodka and bitters.
The windchimes' echo of whatever
Can't be seen. The bottlebrush
Has given up its hundred ghosts,
Each blossom a pinhead firmament,
Galaxies held in place by bristles
That sweep up the pollinated light
In their path along the season.
A scrub jay's Big Bang, the swarming
Dharma of gnats, nothing disturbs
The fixed orders but a reluctant question:
Is the world half-empty or half-full?
Through the leaves, traffic patterns
Bring the interstate to a light
Whose gears a semi seems to shift
With three knife-blade thrusts, angry
To overtake what moves on ahead.
This tree's broken under the day.
The red drips from stem to stem.
That wasn't the question. It was,
Why did we forget to talk about love?
We had all the time in the world.

What we forgot, I heard a voice
Behind me say, was everything else.
Love will leave us alone if we let it.
Besides, the world has no time for us,
The tree no questions of the flower,
One more day no help for all this night.

I wrote "Three Dreams About Elizabeth Bishop" after having indeed dreamed about her. But only the first section of the poem depends on that dream. The dream itself was, as I recall, pretty close to what I describe. What one adds is connective tissue: details that will link together theme and motif, or set up expectations to be fulfilled later on in the poem. So, in this first section, details like "Thanatopsis," beaver-slides, the ghost dance, the foxglove, even the big-diamond-rings crack, all these details were added to give texture or closure to the odd experience of the dream itself. After all, when they are remembered at all, dreams seem vivid but sketchy, and a poem needs to be subtle and complex as well.

Two days after I started writing up this dream—I was living temporarily in Los Angeles at the time—I happened to go to a concert with my late friend Paul Monette. It was in a church. Sitting there, the idea for the second part of the poem occurred to me. Our ideas, says Wordsworth, are made of old feelings. The dead Bishop—did her very name prompt the thought of her as I sat in my pew?—is resurrected in this second section as a guardian angel. Two photographs crossed my mind's eye. In a scrapbook, I have a shot of myself, aged four or five, in shorts, an Eton collar and a cap, standing in front of the family Studebaker. The other photograph sits always beside my desk. Rollie McKenna gave it to me: her shot of Elizabeth in an iron chair, taken in Brazil.

The third section of the poem didn't come for the longest time, though the mention of bottlebrush and the scrub jay tells me I must still have been in California when I wrote it. I had the notion that Elizabeth should slowly withdraw from the poem. So, where in the first section she is prominent, in the second part she makes only a cameo appearance. Now, in the end, she is a disembodied voice. Perhaps that is because here at the end I let my own feelings into the poem, projecting them onto the ghostly figure of the poet. But what I consciously wanted to do here was drive toward the darker side of Bishop's sensibility. The first section highlights the fey, ironic, quizzical, metaphysical side of her imagination. As the poem goes on, I tried to reveal the other side of that bright coin. There is a bitter loneliness to it that I share. Poems about death are poems about love. Poems about love are poems about the imagination. Poems about dreams are poems about death.

WESLEY McNAIR

The recipient of grants from the Rockefeller, Fulbright, and Guggenheim Foundations, Wesley McNair has received an NEH Fellowship in literature and two NEA Fellowships for creative writers. Other honors include the Devins Award (for his volume, *The Faces of Americans in 1853*), the Eunice Tietjens Prize from *Poetry*, the Theodore Roethke Prize from *Poetry Northwest*, and first prize for best annual poem from *Yankee* magazine. Godine recently reissued *The Town of No & My Brother Running*, and has published Mr. McNair's new volume, *Talking in the Dark*. The poet teaches creative writing at the University of Maine at Farmington.

DARK DREAMS, DARK SAYINGS
Poems About Trauma

n part 4 of his well-known poem "The Hill Wife," Robert Frost describes a traumatic event in the life of his central figure, a newly married woman who lives in the isolation of a hill farm. Lying in bed night after night as her husband sleeps, the hill wife watches a "dark pine" outside her window "trying the window latch" of her bedroom. Small as the event is, its recurrence brings repeated and worrisome associations to mind. In a trancelike state before she falls asleep, she imagines that the pine's boughs are "hands," and "a little bird / Before the mystery of glass." Eventually, the tree threatens her in a recurring nightmare, and at the end of Frost's sequence when the hill wife, who seems oddly charmed by fern and black alder at the edge of the clearing, disappears, it is as though the trees have spirited her away.

The story of the hill wife suggests the steps by which psychological trauma often happens: first comes the event that causes the trauma; then, in a response related to dreaming, the traumatized person replays the event, sometimes having actual dreams about it. In the end, the trauma may so trouble the daydreamer and night-dreamer, that he or she is taken over by it.

What went wrong for the hill wife, the psychotherapist might say, is that she never found a way to talk about her problem. Perhaps this is what Frost himself wants to convey in his poem's opening, where he tells us that "she had no saying dark enough / For the dark pine." But I like to think that Frost had the sayings of poetry in mind when he wrote those lines. He was, after all, a poet who often included darkness in his work, and who at the end of his life reportedly kept a light on in his bedroom while he slept, afraid to turn it off. Though the hill wife cannot find the saying that will break the menacing spell of her darkness, it is not hard to imagine that Robert Frost, by using this poem to explore her situation, could for the moment free himself from whatever darkness may have troubled him.

Of course, Frost could not have had his say about the hill wife without the creative process of conjuring her up, which is itself a sort of dreaming, though a more complex sort than the recurrent dreaming associated with the trauma. The poet's dreaming, after all, results in language. Moreover, it brings insight to the thing dreamed, as the compulsive replaying of a traumatic event cannot do. The difference between the two kinds of dreaming was brought home to me when I worked on a poem about a traumatic experience with my stepfather's violence I had as a teenager. I forgot about the experience not long after it happened, but when my stepfather died, it rose up in my memory, and I went over it again and again, evidencing each time, no doubt, the inward stare common to daydreamers—or, in the case of the traumatized, day-marers. One morning at my notebook, having worn the event down to essentials, I started the following poem:

After My Stepfather's Death

Again it is the moment before I left home
for good, and my mother is sitting quietly
in the front seat while my stepfather pulls me
and my suitcase out of the car and begins
hurling my clothes, though now
I notice for the first time how the wind
unfolds my white shirt and puts its slow
arm in the sleeve of my blue shirt and lifts them
all into the air above our heads so beautifully
I want to shout at him to stop and look up
at what he has made, but of course when I turn
to him, a small man, bitter even this young
that the world will not go his way, my stepfather
still moves in his terrible anger, closing the trunk,
and closing himself into the car as hard as he can,
and speeding away into the last years of his life.

No poem is easy to write, but this one was more difficult than most. The big problem was separating the traumatic event I had dreamed from the poem I needed to write about it. In the event, the clothes my angry stepfather threw fell into the roadside ditch or onto hay stubble in the nearby field. I spent at least a month describing the clothes on the ground as I remembered them, but no description seemed to take the poem where it had to go. Putting my poem aside in frustration, I returned to it days later and dreamed the story differently, seeing the clothes opening into the air. Suddenly, they became a means of revealing my stepfather's inner life. Without even mentioning the soap carvings from his childhood I had once found in the house or the drawing from his adolescence that hung in the living room, I was able to speak about the unrealized capacity to create beautiful things I sensed in him, and in that way to intensify our missed connection during his life. Altering the trauma by redreaming it, I went deeper into my relationship with my stepfather than I had ever been, turning what had been a story of pain and fear into a kind of love story. To put it another way, I found a saying dark enough, and full enough, for the experience I once had, and as a result, I was able to dispel some of my trauma's darkness.

While I redreamed the trauma of "After My Stepfather's Death," in another poem, "The Abandonment," I dreamed the details of a traumatic event I never witnessed. The poem describes the heart attack that took my younger brother's life when he was forty-three years old—a heart attack that followed six months of daily running. Eventually, I would write a long poem called, "My Brother Running," attempting to discover what he was running to, and running from. But before I could begin that poem, I had to complete this one which, as it turned out, opened the way to the long poem.

What drew me to "The Abandonment" was not only the terrible news of my brother's death, but the impotence I felt in the face of it. All I had to go on in making my poem about his heart attack were the few facts I had learned from an early morning phone call and the talk at his funeral—these and so much pain that when I sat down to write, what I wanted to utter was a long scream. The poem I ended up with was in one long, ragged sentence:

The Abandonment

Climbing on top of him and breathing
into his mouth this way she could be showing her
desire except that when she draws back
from him to make her little cries
she is turning to her young son just
coming into the room to find his father my brother
on the bed with his eyes closed and the slightest
smile on his lips as if when they
both beat on his chest as they do now
he will come back from the dream he is enjoying
so much he cannot hear her calling his name
louder and louder and the son saying get up
get up discovering both of them discovering
for the first time that all along
he has lived in this body this thing
with shut lids dangling its arms
that have nothing to do with him and everything
they can ever know the wife listening weeping
at his chest and the mute son who will never
forget how she takes the face into her hands now
as if there were nothing in the world
but the face and breathes oh
breathes into the mouth which does not breathe back.

How can a poet, by dreaming deeply into the thing which most troubles him, restore himself? Even knowing from my own writing the power that comes from naming the darkness, I am still amazed by the process. Nevertheless, by using that long sentence to describe my brother's limp body and the attempts by his wife and son to bring him back to life, I was on the way to extricating myself from the news that replayed in my mind. I have already referred to the distinguishing feature of insight in the dreaming of a poem, and as I look back on "The Abandonment," I see how important the insight it offered was to my healing. For the poem helped me to discover a compassion for two actual witnesses who had been devastated by the heart attack, and thus to feel sorrows other than my own. It also led me to an image I returned to in "My Brother Running"—the image, that is, of my brother's smile, which seems to imply he is conscious in some eyes-closed world his wife cannot reach by calling his name and the poem itself cannot reach either, for all of its naming. Whether the smile is really a sign of my brother's presence in this otherworld, or a deceptive last reflex of the face is an unanswered question in the poem, but by imagining that smile and the conspiratorial intimacy it carried for me in life, I found a grim sort of comfort and hope.

In both of the poems I have discussed so far, I began with the bad dream of the trauma, reshaping it into the good, restorative dream of the poem. But in "A Dream of Herman" I put the bad dream aside entirely, replacing it with the poem's good dream. Like the other verses, "A Dream of Herman" was written in response to the death of a family member— my father-in-law Herman, who died in the hospital after a long illness, leaving my wife inconsolable. I didn't need to be told all the details of my wife's bad dreams, waking and sleeping, that followed the event; I had my own troubling dreams. To counter them, I imagined that I had dreamt of a car ride, narrating my poem to suggest I was sharing the dream and its happiness with Diane.

A Dream of Herman

to Diane

I was driving the old Dodge wagon
again, with Coke cans rolling
to the front at stop signs,

and rubbing the dash
every so often to thank the car
for not needing the spare tire
we hadn't fixed. We were on a trip
that felt like going to your father's camp, only
we never got there and didn't care.
It was a beautiful day, just enough wind
coming into the back to make the kids
squint with pure pleasure
as it scribbled their hair, and your mother
patted them, saying what a nice ride it was
in the odd, small voice
she used only for my father.
It was then in the rearview mirror I saw him,
wearing the brown cardigan he always wore
and putting on the shining bell
of his saxophone as if just back
from an intermission. You were smiling,
and suddenly I saw the reason
we were traveling together
and did not want to stop
was Herman, who just sat there
in the cargo space, breathing the scale
until the whole family sat back
in their seats, and then lifted his sax
and opened one more song as wide
and delicate as the floating trees.

As the poem suggests, Herman was a musician, a bandleader who played the saxophone with considerable skill well into his sixties. Yet for all his gifts as a performer, he was a shy and quiet man—the very sort of mortal who might suddenly appear in the cargo space to breathe the scale, delighting my wife and the family once again.

I would like to report that when Diane read "A Dream of Herman," the trauma of her father's death lifted away. The truth is, the poem helped me more than it did her. In a little way, though, it helped her too—not only, I'm guessing, because it showed that Herman was still with us, but because it described family love in a very affirmative way. In its light and affirmation, "A Dream of Herman" is different from the other two poems I have quoted. However, all three deal with fear and sorrow and death, and in each one compassion and love are paramount, making possible the poem's freeing insight, just as Robert Frost's compassion for the hill wife made the insight of his poem sequence possible. Which is to say that in the broadest and best sense, poems about trauma are, like all others, love poems, and their visions give readers the hopeful message that when trauma comes, there are dreams and sayings sufficiently dark, and light, to repel it.

JOYCE CAROL OATES

© MARY CROSS

A prolific novelist, story writer, poet, and essayist,
Joyce Carol Oates won a National Book Award for
her 1969 novel, *them*, at the age of thirty-one. A volume of her poetry, *Anonymous Sins and Other Poems*,
appeared that same year and was swiftly followed by
Love and Its Derangements (1970), *Angel Fire* (1973),
The Fabulous Beasts (1975), and *Women Whose Lives
Are Food, Men Whose Lives Are Money* (1978),
described by one critic as "her darkest work." Oates's
more recent books of poetry include *Invisible Woman:
New and Selected Poems, 1970–1982*, *The Time Trav-
eller: Poems, 1983–1989*, and *Tenderness* (1996). Ms.
Oates lives in Princeton, New Jersey.

"NOSTALGIA"
Dream, Memory, Poetry

These poems are not dreams but the poet's defense against dreams. The terrible power of dreams. The helplessness we feel in the dreamworld, the region of the Other's authority.

My recurring, hypnotic dreams of *back there*—in the world of my childhood and young girlhood in rural upstate New York, in the 1940s and early 1950s. In these dreams I'm somehow not myself, an adult, nor even a child, but a sort of bodiless quivering ectoplasm lacking personhood, personality, but gifted with an extraordinary capacity for *seeing*. As if everything is magnified, vivid and sharpened.

The "I"-narrators of the linked poems are coherent, ironic commentators, but the actual dreams lack intellect, and are absolutely silent. Instead of the self I recognize as me, there is a force field of raw, unmediated emotion. Usually, as in most dreams of mine, a single image dominates: the abandoned old one-room schoolhouse I attended through five tumultuous grades, for instance. Or the landscape, the very atmosphere of the countryside I loved so much as a child without knowing it was "love" I felt, so deep and wholly unquestioned was my bond with it. For some reason, my dreams of *back there* are virtually always unpopulated. The predominant sensation is one of keen, melancholy loneliness. (Though in fact I was the elder, much loved and rather spoiled child of young, attractive, vigorous parents who lived with my mother's adoptive parents on their farm—a crowded household.) This would seem to be the yearning of the dreamer for the object of his or her dream, of which the dream-phantasm is itself but a simulacrum. The mysterious vision that, generated from within the brain, is nonetheless inaccessible even as we approach it.

We don't know to what extent we who are writers write under the direction of the dreaming self, the Other. Sometimes we imagine ourselves autonomous, consciously and craftily inventive; at other times, staggering with the aftershock of a night of profound, disturbing dreams, we understand that, like Lear, we but slenderly know ourselves, and are humbly grateful that we can navigate our pitching, careening little boats as well as we do. My pride in my volitional self frequently goes before a fall, or a collapse, in the shifting hallucinatory region of my dreams.

The poems "The Lord Is My Shepherd, I Shall Not Want" and "Nostalgia" were written several years ago, but they seem so immediate to me they might have been written yesterday. The dreams that generated them are recurring, even obsessive dreams, not of incidents or of people, at least not directly, but of that lost world *back there*. The setting for the poems is a fictitious "Ransomville," however—not Millersport, New York, where my grandparents' small farm was located. (Millersport is a crossroads rural community twenty miles north of Buffalo, lacking a post office, as it lacks any discernible center; it seems to have shrunken over the decades, and my parents who live on the same plot of land they lived on as newlyweds have fewer neighbors now! There is in fact another village called Ransomville in the adjoining county, but the "Ransomville" of the poems is not that Ransomville. It's solely the name—the "ransom" at the core of the "ville"—that appeals.) Here I am, in "Nostalgia," contemplating the old schoolhouse on the unpaved Tonawanda Creek Road, about a mile from my home; this first school of mine, in my child's highly wrought imagination, a temple of sorts, a place of intense excitement, apprehension, dread. Inside, I was singled out as a star in first grade (quite literally amassing, over the course of five years, any number of tiny red stars pasted beside my name on the spelling bee chart affixed to the wall); outside, going to and from school, and often in the schoolyard itself, I was, in the company of other small children, or alone, at the mercy (if "mercy" isn't an ironic term here) of older boys. (Like most rural schools of its type, District No. 7 consisted of eight grades, and the disparity in ages, sizes, behavior among the students was considerable.) The schoolhouse, a crudely shingled cooplike structure set cellarless upon a stone foundation, on a slope above the Tonawanda Creek, seemed to have been there forever, not newly built when my mother, born 1917, attended it as a girl, and altered only minimally in the intervening years. Inside were rows of desks increasing in size from front to back, attached at the bottom by runners, like toboggans; a woodburning iron stove that was our sole source of heat (this, in upstate New York where winter temperatures commonly dropped below zero), tended by our heroic teacher, Mrs. Dietz; no indoor plumbing of course, only ghastly smelly unheated outhouses at the rear—the boys' to the left, the girls' to the right. At the front of the school was a weedy, cindery schoolyard of sorts, surrounded by open fields; curious ravines and humps in the earth, as if some ancient violence had been committed against it. There was an unnerving optical illusion about the schoolhouse: built on a rise, its crude stone foundation bearing it aloft, it appeared much higher at the rear than at the front.

Nietzsche, the poet of inconstancy, has observed that nothing is truly fixed: not merely is the form of expression always fluid, but content as well—"meaning." So meaning is a function of perspective and perspective is temporal more often than spatial: where, as young children, savagely bullied and threatened by older, stronger, crueller children, in fact adolescents, dwarf-adults, we experience fear, ignominy, hurt, shame—for all victims, even nine-year-old girls, are imbued with shame—with the passage of time we come to see how such experiences allow us sympathy with others similarly, or more savagely, violated; and who, if we are to speak honestly, has not been "violated"? To survive a rural childhood of this sort, far from the enforced gentility of suburban America in the 1950s, is to look back upon a virtual allegory of man's inhumanity to man, in miniature. *Tragedy breaks down the dykes between human beings*, Yeats has said. And even hurt less extreme than tragedy can be powerfully, unforgettably illuminating.

(Talk to me of mass violence!—Serbian atrocities against civilians, tribal massacres in Africa, the "rape of Nanking" and the high-tech ingenuities of the Nazi holocaust! Out of certain experiences of my background in "rural America" have sprung, I've wryly observed, my conviction that the austere, intransigent vision of Charles Darwin is finally the only philosophy that isn't sentimental or deluded. Darwin's theory of "natural selection"—not a purposeful but a random, wayward, blind and wholly contingent evolutionary drive, a crazed blizzard of competing DNA codes each generated by its individual god—is at once the simplest and the most eloquent of all ideologies. Not acts of evil but acts of goodness, generosity, enlightenment are what surprise me. Before I was eleven years old and sent to the small city of Lockport, seven miles away, to attend a genteel suburban elementary school as a sixth grader, I'd learned not to expect mercy from my tormentors, and, for a girl, to run very fast.)

In these poems, which are not at all confessional, nor even personal, virtually none of this is present. Perhaps such convictions, like the memories that generate them, shimmer at the edges of strategies of language; the poem is a species of magic, undertaken for its own lyric eloquence and bravado, like any "artwork," but also for purposes of catharsis and exorcism. Does such magic work, in pragmatic psychological terms? *Should* it work? Perhaps the very essence of our inner lives, hidden from others, is obsession, hauntedness: as in the natural cycle of sleep, waking sleep, waking, we continually discover ourselves in different guises yet always ineluctably ourselves. What does it mean, after all, that a writer, like a dreamer, is compelled to return again and again to a certain landscape, a certain time? What expenditures of spirit are required to evoke emotionally, in seemingly neutral images, that which cannot be directly expressed? In the equation of my (girl's) life *back there* there is

always an *x*. It will always remain an *x*. I will not speak of it directly, perhaps could not, as one can't stare for long into a blinding light. I don't
mean this as subterfuge or coyness or even as a sort of "universal" code;
I'm doubtful of the language of victim-survivors and hesitant to make, in
this case as elsewhere, abstract claims.

Some days are solar, others lunar. By which I mean there are days
when we're fully conscious of our motivations, our decisions, our behavior; and there are other days when we stagger from our dreams as from a
seismic upheaval that leaves us shaken for hours. A certain percentage of
my dreams exert an eerie, almost terrifying authority over me, so that I
seem to be in thrall to their aftershock, exhausted through much of the
morning, sometimes through an entire day. I know myself in thrall to—
what? These images, these emotions, in themselves unspeakable, which
must be transposed into strategies of words (my minimal definition of
both poetry and prose as genres) in order to be contemplated at all.

I love it, the eye lifting skyward to nothing is the adult claim of
control over the emotions generated by childhood experience, and therefore a triumph of a kind—if triumph belated by decades is truly a triumph. So too the defiant claim, *I wasn't one of them, I escaped early. / I
never believed.* (If the "I" is the poet, and not wholly a fictitious narrator,
this both is and is not true, for I left home for college at the age of eighteen and never really returned for any sustained period of time, yet of
course we carry "home" with us, and any claim of "escape" is doubtful.)
To say that I'm haunted by my past, at least certain inassimilable aspects
of my past, is to say nothing out of the ordinary, nothing that distin-
guishes me from most other individuals; all that might distinguish me, for
better or worse, is that I've fashioned so much of my past into language—
"artful strategies of words."

A fundamental truth of my life is: I loved my parents, yet they
were unable to protect me from much that surrounded me, nor were they

even very clearly aware of it, for of course I could not speak of it, as adults are unaware of the intense, secret inner lives of their own children. (As children are unaware of their parents' secret lives.) Out of this paradox has come much of my writing, and so I credit it with my very identity, my innermost being. There are mornings following dreams when my eyes flood tears. A thin, smarting, sourceless and inexhaustible stream of tears. I have learned to ignore the tears, which seem to have no organic basis, and continue with my life, my work. I make it a point to *see through* the tears that, in other circumstances, might blind me. Noticing my reddened eyes, someone might inquire if I've been crying?—but of course I haven't been crying, why should I have been crying? I'm not *back there*.

The Lord Is My Shepherd, I Shall Not Want

In August, in upstate New York,
summer turns sullen.
Blacktop highways sticky as licorice.
Red earth cracked like an old farmer's hands.

One by one they left the high stone house
    of their ancestors.
One by one entering the graveyard tottering
    downhill behind the Ransomville Lutheran Church.

I wasn't one of them, I escaped early.
I never believed.
I don't believe anything anyone has ever told me.
I wouldn't believe even you if you swore to me
    the deepest truth of your tinsel heart.

Nostalgia
Rural District School #7, Ransomville, New York

Crumbling stone steps of the old schoolhouse
Boarded-up windows   shards of winking glass
Built 1898, numerals faint in stone as shadow
Through a window, obedient rows of desks   mute

How many generations of this rocky countryside grown & gone
How many memories   & all forgotten
& soon to be razed   & goodbye America
The flagless pole, what relief!
I love it, the eye lifting skyward   to nothing
Never to pledge allegiance to the United States of America
    again
Never to press my flat right hand over my heart again
    as if I had one

DAVID RAY

JUDY RAY

From David Ray's first book, *X-Rays: A Book of Poems* (1965), to his recent *Kangaroo Paws* (1995), the poet draws on deeply personal encounters with the world. These include his childhood experiences in an orphanage, the death of his son, and his extensive travels with his wife, poet Judy Ray. He won the Maurice English Award in 1988, was twice the recipient of the William Carlos Williams Award, and in 1997 received the Allen Ginsberg Award. He lived in Kansas City for many years where he taught at the University of Missouri and edited the journal *New Letters*. He and his wife moved recently to Tucson, Arizona.

DREAMWORK, GRIEFWORK, POEMWORK

From the day we visited the Uffizi in Florence and bought a postcard of the Bronzino painting that looked just like Sam, a postcard which I taped on the wooden panel above and behind the front seat of the Volkswagen van in which we had wandered and slept, I thought of my son as that Renaissance boy with a feather—and even then there was sometimes a grief, a poignant anxiety in my regard of him, as if his life had another dimension, extending beyond our time together.

Even in his infancy, this awareness had animated poems about Sam, which seemed like gifts he had given me. These poems always broke free of the scene before me—whether it was looking down upon Sam as he slept in his crib or stood in his stroller or came running with such a gift as a peacock feather—and they clearly made reference to this larger mystery. I could go no farther than a reference—for I did not understand, only sensed, the dimension beyond. After his death, when I experienced this dimension with more clarity, as if a door to another world is opened by crisis, I soon learned that it was a mistake to try—except in the work of poems, dreams, and meditation—to explain this feeling, both inspiring and bewildering, to others.

Like any other spiritual experience, my faith that my son's life had a larger meaning than that framed by his nineteen years on earth was for the most part ineffable. I quickly learned that I could either *experience* this sense of connection from this shore of life to the one beyond in all its isolate and exiling loneliness, or I could frustrate myself with the futility of "rational" understanding and attempting to share the experience with others.

It is refreshing to read Carl Jung and other rebels against traditional logic, with their consequent research into synchronicity and other phenomena. Even the dedicatedly imagist poem only comes alive if the sense of something beyond the apparent informs it. What would "The Red Wheelbarrow" be without the never-defined "So much" upon which both the poet's perception and the satori depend? Like a blind man who can run without harm through a forest, bumping into a tree only if he starts to question this ability, we pay a price when we lose faith with the world given us—every word of it.

Gifts of dreams can be carried directly and laid upon the altar of the poem. And a crisis such as grief—a form of deep and loyal and abiding love—opens the door beyond our first five senses. A poet would have to put up very powerful resistance indeed not to catch some of this agitation in his work. *Sam's Book* is the tip of an iceberg that is itself the tip of an iceberg—a few poems that represent many others that caught some of the knife-sharp edges of grief's stormy sea. The process is ongoing, for I've not spooned out that sea. No poem resolves grief, any more than it resolves any other form of love, but the writing itself can provide a ritual and a reason for survival. For me it was something to hang on to, and I felt a duty to seek truth through "writing as prayer," which is what it was for Kafka.

If we believe that chaos can be organized at all—or that it is already held together by some sort of sublimity—we must also believe that our seeking must go beyond surfaces. To me, faith in that process of seeking is the commitment of both dream and poem, whether they succeed or fail by anybody's definition. The dream opens a door to a world of symbolism that speaks more directly—and both more boldly and more subtly—than words. Thus is energized a dialogue between two worlds— that of the newly discovered and the forever known, between the mind's great power in the dream and its helplessness in the outer world, between the vast spaces ruled by the ancient gods willing to pass on their secrets and our puny ignorance in this life. Those who have grabbed at the offerings in dreams probably include Lucretius, who wrote down an accurate description of atomic structure, many who have made other scientific discoveries (the DNA helix, for example), and the ancient artist who in a cave in Spain left illustrations for a modern embryology text—womb with homunculus within along with a series of six eggs, a series showing cell division in stages.

Of such apparent prescience, the viewer who responds to the language of symbolism may well accept an image as valid, trusting that if it speaks to him, its message is worth hearing, and may be evidence of a structure and harmony in nature too resonant and profound to be nothing but lies, chimeras, fantasies. It is, quite simply, a matter of accepting on faith or not at all—of opposing the apparent with as much resistance as materialists and atheists have to faith itself. The poet is, perhaps, among the least likely to offer resistance to the image given by dreaming. He is willing to leave the job of opposing faith in the numinous to those obliged to prove their rationality at all times.

Again and again after my son's death, and even long before, there were strong hints of fatality, accident, and of the inevitability of loss, when "my son too would / have his day / and be gone" ("In the Art Museum," *Dragging the Main*, 1968). In the poem about our visit to Paestum there is a reference to his ancient sandals, which had helped wear down the stone steps of the temple. Again and again I had seen his life as one of the immortals. Asleep in his crib, thumb in mouth, he was nonetheless an ancient man, his destiny inseparable from that of the tragic earth. Standing up in his stroller, he was "drunk with enthusiasm for a sick world." There was a mystery I never doubted, though I did not presume to understand it. His natural wisdom was seldom if ever limited to his years.

Buddhists tell us that the soul is reborn within forty-nine days, and in my poem about Bhopal, the catastrophe that happened three months after my Sam's death, I speculated about the possibility that he had already gone on to another life:

> In fact he might have gone on
> to Bhopal just in time to die again
> at just three months. Not likely, but who knows?
>
> (*Sam's Book*, p. 72)

He had clearly entered his life of nineteen years with so much spirit that it had to come from other lives completed, and I had many signs that he was on his way from this one. Strangely, this did not mitigate grief, for I blamed myself. A man cannot take credit for the success of his children, but it is another matter with disasters.

From the poem I wrote on the night of his birth and another describing that birth, his life had always been reflected in these subliminally apprehended markers, and even there a restlessness to accomplish his mission in life and depart was so strongly hinted that it could be overlooked only as I for six weeks failed to notice, on an antique French lamp by our bedside, a light-switch that had been glowing through day and night with a long forbidden infusion of radium.

Whatever the dark forces that grabbed my son on that night in the fall of 1984, circumstances that were never fully clear—his accidental death after a night of drinking with his Carleton College classmates—it was the worst thing that ever happened in my life as well, and it opened even very old childhood losses and traumas as if time had never healed over with even the scar of a single molecule's thickness. Spinoza's Proposition 18, in his *Ethics*, is absolutely accurate: "A man is affected by the image of a past or future thing with the same emotion of joy or sorrow as that with which he is affected by the image of a present thing. . . . The body is affected by the image of the thing in the same way as if the thing itself were present." Grief subsides but does not disappear—it is merely in time "not so constant," as it is "generally disturbed by the images of other things." Spinoza's next Proposition begins: "He who imagines what he loves is destroyed will sorrow."

Grief is supposedly experienced in neat stages, and it is to many an offense against good taste if survivors do not deport themselves according to the socially permissible expectations. Some tears are, perhaps, understandable. Rage arouses fear in the bourgeois heart and defines the angry survivor as an enemy of the people. And yet the perceptive Boccaccio long ago defined anger as "nothing but a sudden and unreflecting emotion aroused by the grief we feel, which expels our reason, blinds the eyes of the spirit with darkness, and consumes our souls with burning rage" (*The Decameron*, Fourth Day, Third Tale). How differently we might deal with anger if we recognized the grief behind it!

My grief changed everything in my life, and changed it permanently. Relationships were bitterly shifted, as if rocks had tumbled into the sea, for friend was not there for friend, neighbor for neighbor, colleague for colleague, and society's rituals were once again deficient. And because this grief exponentially increased my isolation and exile from others, my rejection by many who turned away—out of their refusal to face their own fears, perhaps, if one must take on the burden of making excuses for them—I have found hard to forgive. It was as if various individuals were in a contest to demonstrate excellence in the fine art of insensitivity.

A year into the second decade of grieving for Sam, I still await the humility Gregory Bateson describes: ". . . there is, I think, a stage which I can only dimly envisage, where pessimism and anger are replaced by something else—perhaps humility. And from this stage onward to whatever other stages there may be, there is loneliness." Alan Watts, quoting this passage in *Psychotherapy East and West*, adds:

> This is the loneliness of liberation, of no longer finding security by taking sides with the crowd, of no longer believing that the rules of the game are the laws of nature. . . . Liberation begins from the point where anxiety or guilt becomes insupportable,

where the individual feels that he can no longer tolerate his situation as an ego in opposition to an alien society, to a universe in which pain and death deny him, or to negative emotions which overwhelm him. Ordinarily, he is quite unaware of the fact that his distress arises from a contradiction in the rules of the social game. He blames God, or other people, or even himself—but none of these are responsible. There has simply been a mistake whose consequences no one could have foreseen—a wrong step in biological adaptation which, presumably, seemed at first to be very promising. (129)

Our ultimate egotism, then, is to fail to grasp the possibility of randomness and the absurd as they strike ourselves and our loved ones. To acknowledge such a reality would, after all, be to deny our importance in the cosmos. We could no longer put ourselves in the center of anything, even grief.

And we must go on listening to our dreams, for as L. L. Whyte reminded us, our lives are an "unconscious process with conscious aspects." It is the dream that speaks from our deepest center and that can unlock and liberate. The poem is altar for the dream.

"The Return" emerged from my grief, but it is inseparable from the total experience, including my reading widely to seek answers others found in ages past. The poem was, perhaps, prompted almost as much by my serendipitous reading of the Shelley passage as by the dream described, for I had long known in the abstract that living wholly and without reserve in the present was the key to sanity and liberation from grief and regrets, guilt and woe about past, fear about future. But Shelley said it well—the demon rocks the heart off balance when the guardian angel of such wisdom is not alert. That we must live in the present or die holds true, and in this event it is acceptable to live in the present *and* die, for death is not denied its place. (Someone remarked that his ambition

was to be alive until he dies. So few of us are. And it was Seneca who
wrote centuries ago that "the part of life we live is short. All the rest is
not life, but merely time.")

Sam's face was very vivid in the dream that became "The
Return," and it was a recognition of his changed status, his powers as an
angel, that he should have come from the airport instantaneously. (My
years-earlier poem "On a Fifteenth Century Angel" had pondered the
mystery of these abstractions that yet seemed very real when the angels
portrayed—this one by Gerard David—had ruddy cheeks and a mace
used to crack a nodding noggin.) Now, if there were angels, Sam was such
a one and, ironically, would have acquired an invulnerability he did not
have in life—though teenagers are notorious for taking risks and presum-
ing guaranteed safe conduct. When Sam and his sister, Wesley, had come
for visits, I had met them at the airport, often in snow or storm, anxious.
Sometimes the plane was late, sometimes very late. Such worry was need-
less.

And yet the anxious parent in both pride and bewilderment goes
on fretting, and the death of a child leaves a permanent hypersensitivity
to danger, which others mock. I glance at a playground slide and remember the day in Bari when Sam fell off and cut his upper lip—I did not
catch him in time. I glance at a gate where he waterproofed the wood
with a chemical (lindane) I later found was terribly toxic, and I accuse
myself of negligence, though any harm done by those vapors has become
irrelevant.

Yet I fear that monster who gave you a ride.
What abduction was that, what crime on the way?

The boy's life was taken by dark forces—snatched in the night as
if by a demon, a murderous kidnapper—and yet the poem grabs at hope
for his future life and appreciation of the joy he had, as when he hugged

the rain-darkened bark of a tree that winter we lived on a farm in York-
shire. He often said, as some of my other poems have recorded, things
that were preternatural with wisdom or insight. (I will never entirely
believe we simply read meanings *into* these gifts.) That he wanted "to be
born again out of the corn" was a deeply felt wish which he voiced. Perhaps he never intended or was meant to be with us beyond nineteen
years. The world and its realities beneath the surfaces are so much vaster
than we are that it is arrogance itself (or ego, from which we need liberation) even to look for cause and effect. Sam's arrival and departure were
mysteries and ever will be. If I ever break free of the bondage of fear and
false knowledge taught me by my culture, it will be largely from Sam's
leading me—in the words of Judy Ray's poem—"where you had thought
to lead."

"The Return" was important to me, as have been both published
and unpublished griefwork poems, because writing gave me something to
hang onto at a time when I felt that I had been cut in two, as if by a samu-
rai's sword. I am still not whole again, but the waves of grief subside to a
tolerable level, and though Shelley's "guardian angel" departs, he sometimes returns for a visit, and helps me live in the present.

Lately, after a long period of my being out of touch with
dreams—possibly as a result of antidepressant medication—Sam has
made new visitations. Eleven years after his death I returned to France,
near the village where my wife and I were when we learned of his death.
As this was the place the loss happened to me, if not to him, grief flared
up with fresh intensity. And the dreams returned like a monsoon. At first
I was bothered with more self-blame for not having made more progress
in distancing myself from an event that was, after all, eleven years ago.
But surely it is better (less sick) to be in touch with the grief than out of
touch, for it is a reality even if it is beyond the awareness or scope of others. If thirty-four years were not enough for Tennyson to grieve, should
eleven be reason to condemn myself?

The shock Gregory Bateson describes is not so easily dissipated—from any event that happens outside the rules of life as you know them, any event you cannot fit into your philosophy. Indeed, the rules themselves are suddenly changed, as they are in war. Words, inadequate to deal with several emotions at once, must give way to the chaos of trauma in which perhaps a thousand emotions are caught like detritus in a spinning tornado. All poems, like the remembered shards of rich and vivid dreams, are mere fragments of the total experience, whether or not they have been eroded by time.

In the recent dreams, I think I have acknowledged that Sam is truly gone, though I still stare after children who look like him, as if he might have returned in life as in dream. From a distance I examine a child's face closely, as if there's still a chance it's Sam. But then he gazes at me, from deep shadows, a darkness on his face, more likely now of stone than flesh. And then I know.

We would not be the first to feel gratitude for the gift of dreams, which help us sort out the chaos and confusion of our lives, to process and rearrange a day until it can be lived with. Hard work goes on in dreams, and in trying to hear what they say to us. Poems like "The Return" are merely a part of that work and of the continuing labor of grief, which I am more realistic about now than at any time since Sam's death. For I have finally realized the simple truth Scott Fitzgerald described in *Tender Is the Night:*

> One writes of scars healed, a loose parallel to the pathology of the skin, but there is no such thing in the life of an individual. There are open wounds, shrunk sometimes to the size of a pin-prick, but wounds still. The marks of suffering are more comparable to the loss of a finger, or of the sight of an eye. We may not miss them, either, for one minute in a year, but if we should there is nothing to be done about it.

We can understand others only through their grief, not by block-
ing our awareness of it, or forbidding their expression of it. And we can
understand ourselves only through being open to the dream, and what
the late poet Stanley Cooperman called "poeming" is one of several valid
ways to serve the dream.

The Return

The past and future were forgot
As they had been, and would be, not. —
But soon, the guardian angel gone,
The demon reassumed his throne
In my faint heart.

Shelley

First visitation in a dream: you're back
with bags in hand, through screen door greeted.
And how did you make it back so fast, I ask.
You say you flew, got a ride from the airport.
So I think of that wondrous flight through skies,
snow blown in winds, great clouds tumbling, luminous,
and the landing as an angel might have it,
touching ground, then wobbling to steady himself.
Yet I fear that monster who gave you a ride.
What abduction was that, what crime on the way?
Still, I wake happy to have this small blessing.
And recall how at four you hugged the dark trees,
how you said you wanted to be born again, out of the corn.

PATRICIA TRAXLER

RUTH MORITZ

Born and raised in San Diego, Patricia Traxler has published three books of poetry: *Blood Calendar*, *The Glass Woman*, and *Forbidden Words*. She received two successive Bunting Fellowships at Radcliffe and served as the 1996 Hugo Poet at the University of Montana and as the 1997 Thurber Poet at Ohio State. Her work was selected by A. R. Ammons for inclusion in *Best American Poetry, 1994*. Currently living in Kansas, Traxler is poet-in-residence at a large regional hospital where she provides writing therapies for mental health patients. She is completing work on her fourth collection of poems, *Paradise Notes*.

THE UNREMEMBERED DREAM

"**I**f you ever see a pile of dirty laundry in a dream," I heard my Irish grandmother caution my mother when I was a kid, "it means your life will soon be at sixes and sevens." By the ominous tone in Gran's voice, and by the way my mother's fingers grazed her own throat then, I knew that whatever "at sixes and sevens" meant, it couldn't be good. "A pile of *clean* laundry, though," Gran added in a lighter tone, "*that* foretells an improvement in your life, a return to order and stability." *Whew.*

It seemed to me that my grandmother was always instructing her daughters in the language of dreams and the necessity to heed it if you knew what was good for you. Whenever possible, I eavesdropped while Gran talked to my mother and my aunts, and I would carry the arcane tidbits I collected back to my bedroom where I mused upon them at night after my three younger sisters had fallen asleep in the beds around me.

My grandmother was a poet from County Cork—a skinny, acerbic, witty woman with wide and eventful blue eyes, high cheekbones, and a long grey braid she wore twisted into a knot behind her neck during the day. In the years when she lived with us her poetry was a force in our household, as were her regular pronouncements about the mystical, the mysterious, and the unseen. As a child I thought of her poetry as *allied* with those other elements, part of a continuum, connected in some irrefutable and unknowable way to all that was magical or dangerous, or both. Somewhere along the line I came to see dreams as the provenance of poetry, a sort of ethereal bog where poems dwelt beneath the surface and you could fish them out at your own peril.

In childhood and through my teens I would listen, rapt, whenever Gran and Mama and my aunts Marjorie and Jane described to one another the dreams they'd had the previous night. In recounting any dream, the women of our family used the same tones—hushed, intense, always lyrical—that they might use to recite a poem, and when one of them had finished the telling, the others would breathe out a soft collective *oh,* as if the dreamer had found—or *made*—a thing of beauty, insight, or awesome ominousness. Then, after a decent interval, they would all jump in to offer up—and argue—the interpretive possibilities of the dream just recounted. To me, often snooping from behind a door or a piece of furniture, it was fascinating, if a little scary. And it made me wonder if *not* to dream one night could be construed as a failure of the imagination.

I guess it was inevitable that I should come to regard dreams not only as poetry bogs and as reservoirs of insight, knowledge, and foretelling, but also as creations to be proud of. I was around twelve when my dreams began to show up already *titled.* Among them I recall "The Hairy Hand," "The Quilted Foot," "Dinner with Two Men in the Rocking House," and what I believe was the last of my dreams to have a title—"The Stained Glass Hummingbird in the Cathedral at High Mass at High Noon." (I wouldn't like to see these titles undergo any Freudian scrutiny.)

By the time I began to publish my poetry, I'd long since come to terms with the part that dreams can play in the making of a poem. And it wasn't usually those dreams I could *recall* that informed and nourished my poems. It was the dreams I had no access to—the dreams I could not remember.

In my mind, dreams are divided into two essential categories. First, there's the sort of dream that lives on so clear and specific in memory that you can describe it to someone in detail the next day or even for years afterward; the dream from which you can mine truths that give valuable insight into yourself, your life, and even, some would say, your future. No matter how beautifully wrought, this is ultimately a utilitarian dream—a tool or resource useful and beneficial to your everyday existence. Occasionally this sort of dream may give rise to a poem, or an image for a poem, but this doesn't seem to be its raison d'être.

Then there's the second variety of dream—the dream from which you wake shaken or deeply moved, but which you can't quite recall in specific. You look around the room in the half-light and everything once familiar now seems to exist in the wake of some enormous sound or stir just past, an event you can't quite identify. All day you remain in the sway of this unremembered dream, at times believing you're about to retrieve it intact from the bog, but always it stays beyond reach—just beyond reach.

It's this unremembered dream which roots most deeply in the mind and soul of the poet—this dream we can't fully waken from till we've brought it into our waking life and through poetry rendered it incarnate. It may be precisely *because* we don't remember a dream—*can't* remember it—that it captures our imaginations, inspires in us a longing, a striving to retrieve what has been lost to us before we ever had it. We may not consciously acknowledge the dream as the source of this longing, but in some way we recognize that to feel whole again we must retrieve it and reconstitute it in words. Poets struggle for lifetimes with that glimmer and echo, pulling half-formed images from the chiaroscuro of our imaginations and wrestling them onto the page, always at the mercy of language.

Throughout childhood I often stood in the doorway and watched my grandmother as she ran a pen across the pages of a green clothbound journal in her cluttered room far at the back of our house. I knew better than to speak to her when she was writing poetry. She'd warned me often enough about how very easy it is to lose a poem, "how fast a poem can fly." As I watched her there, I knew she'd drifted off somewhere far beyond our little life on Wightman Street in San Diego and was wandering in that distant place alone, trying to find her way to what she could almost see, almost hear, almost name.

"If you dream you're falling and you don't wake up before you land, you'll die," I'd heard my mother say, no doubt repeating something her mother had told her. In some reversal of that old wives' tale, when I was a child it seemed to me that if I interrupted my grandmother when she was writing she might be lost to me forever, stranded somewhere between terra firma and heaven.

To me it's always made perfect sense that the woman who gave me poetry was also the person who taught me to attend to dreams. Just after waking each day, and when I turn inward again to make my way back through the luminous or umbrous tangle of images that populate dreams, I'm not overly disappointed if I can't immediately retrieve a dream whose presence haunts me. I know it means I've been given the seed of another poem, and that in the coming days and nights my job will be to tend it and coax it into being. Sometimes I succeed.

For any poet a dream can be a summons, the eternally renewed directive that blooms while we sleep. Who knows how many of the poems we love to read were first seeded there? And who can say how often a poet writes to retrieve the unremembered dream?

DIANE WAKOSKI

PHOTOGRAPH BY ROBERT TURNEY

Diane Wakoski grew up in Southern California, lived in New York City for the decade of the 1960s, and now lives in East Lansing, Michigan, where she has been the writer-in-residence at Michigan State University for over twenty years. Her selected poems *Emerald Ice* won the William Carlos Williams Prize in 1989. She has published more than twenty collections of poems, from *Coins & Coffins* (1962) to *Argonaut Rose* (1997).

HOW MY GREEN SILK DREAMS LED TO THE CONCEPT OF PERSONAL MYTHOLOGY

very night I would dream a kind of continuing story, somewhat fairy-tale-like, of romance or sex, and in all the dreams the floor was covered with green silk, bolts of it, rippled and stiff like taffeta, and I often could remember nothing about the people in the dream, or what actually happened, though the aftereffect was of eroticism. But I always remembered the green silk.

This was in the late 1950s, when I was an undergraduate at Berkeley, living in an apartment on Telegraph Avenue with a very exotic music-major roommate, who smoked cigarettes in a cigarette holder, and in fact had a green carpet on the floor of her room, though I myself had tatami mats of light straw on my own. I was a very serious young poet at that time trying, by writing poems, to find a way to cope with my sense of loss, my loneliness, my longing for a perfect lover and the world of beautiful, artful things. I did not believe that anything in my life was interesting enough to write about. In fact, I thought that the only even mildly interesting stories about me were simply shameful ones, and while I needed to tell them, I also needed to keep my shame(s) a secret. I imagine that is probably one of the reasons I was so attracted to surrealism and the idea of dream imagery. It was a way to disguise the secrets of one's life, while telling them through fantastic or artful images and actions.

Sometimes I would borrow a green glass ring that my exotic roommate had in her jewelry box, and wear it while I made little water colors. I have virtually no talent as a visual artist, but for some reason I found myself attracted to making water colors once in a while. I never did this unless I was wearing Adele's green ring and I believe that when I did so, I entered into the world of the green silk dreams. None of my poems from that undergraduate period, many of which were published in my first chap book, *Coins & Coffins*, came specifically out of the dreams. However, what thinking about and occasionally writing down the dreams did for me was to make me aware of dream imagery as identical to what Jerome Rothenberg and Robert Kelly were later to call "deep image," in their search for a new poetics derived from archetypal patterns.

As a child, I was magnetized by color, vivid color, primary colors, particularly blue and yellow. I suppose my almost primal love for these colors must come somewhat out of my Southern California landscape, the sapphire blue of the Pacific Ocean on a sun-clear day, the golden yellow of so many of the flowers like the hillside lupine, the lemons and the ripening oranges in the citrus groves, and also the dark yellow orange of the California poppies, the brownish yellow of the bare hills. I always claimed that blue was my favorite color, and deep blues have always had a kind of mesmerizing effect on me. In retrospect I have wondered, once I started dreaming in color, for those green silk dreams are rare among my dreams which usually are not in color, why it wasn't bolts of blue silk covering my dream floor? Perhaps the rationale of the unconscious mind put the blue and yellow of my childhood landscape together and produced green? Perhaps it was simply archetypal, and green is the color of creativity, of new plant life, and these dreams signaled the birth of my new deep image, dream-inspired poetry life?

When I moved to New York City with composer La Monte Young, in the autumn of 1960, I continued writing out of this fantastic kind of dream-inspired imagery. The title of my first book of poems, from the title poem in it, "Coins & Coffins," published by Jerome Rothenberg's Hawk's Well Press as an example of deep image poetry, alludes to symbols from the tarot deck. But it also begins to showcase a totemic image for me, right out of my green silk dream history, the ring. Of course, for me, rings symbolize marriage, the devotion of the husband and lover which I have so longed for, and which until middle age eluded me in any successful way. The poem also contains an early version of my embrace of gold and silver images, the oranges' gold, and another totemic image for me, the key, which in the poem becomes the image of silver keys.

The key is used to introduce the revelation of the poem, that the key is the trope which turns the poem to the image of the key ring and thus the source of death. The final lines read:

> And I am trying to believe, I haven't seen glinting through
> the leaves,
> the hanged man,
> caught by his key ring—
> hanged by the key,
> and the sun catching it, as he swings.

The green, of my Green Silk Dreams, is to evolve over the years, in my poems, into a bevy of plant and gardening images, particularly focused on flowers, usually brilliant ones like the crimson amaryllis, which for me is an image of a bloody lily, death and life together. But the next use of specific dreams that occurred in my continuing exploration of the deep image came in the form of a character whom I either actually dreamed, or invented as a result of a dream. Her name is Jennifer Snow, and of course she is a version of Diane. In my dream, she looked like a fellow undergraduate at Berkeley, Ann Yothers, who was slim and very goddesslike in her blondness. She was also a brilliant student and seemed terribly in control of her life as a studious kind of beauty, and I am sure that I wished I could be her, though desperately I held to myself the belief that I wrote better poems than she did.

I guess this is the way the imagination works, or mine does, anyway. I saw a person in real life who had qualities that I wanted to claim, so I invented Jennifer Snow who looked like her and had those qualities, but was really me. The name Snow is also part of my own fairy-tale mythology. How I, the passionate person, always in thrall to my hair-trigger emotions, always out of control, longed to be the icy Snow Queen, cool and reserved, beautiful and untouched by all the dramas and dangers

I felt beset my life. I also had moved from California where I had grown up not seeing snow, to New York City where, during the first winter of my almost fifteen-year residence there, a snowstorm so huge fell on Manhattan that all the businesses shut down for a day. I was living in New York City without a winter coat or boots, and I certainly experienced the snow in a terrifying way that year. I wanted, I suppose, to be the snow or at least the Snow Queen, and thus immune to its punishments.

In my 1966 Doubleday book, I published the poem first written out of the Jennifer Snow dream experiences, "The Five Dreams of Jennifer Snow and Her Testament." This is another somewhat seminal poem for me, in that it names many of the images that have become a regular part of my mythic iconography: the lion, Death (as the figure of a man), the cup, the mirror, water, a horse, cars, fish, gems/diamonds and jade, Spain, spiders, card games and birds. The poem chronicles a kind of dreamlike encounter that Jennifer Snow has with Death, but also presents all these images as dream images which are the real life of Jennifer Snow, whereas her waking life is simply an encounter with Death. I believe this poem focuses on a vision of life that persists throughout all my poems, that the waking life is not nearly as important as the dream life, or the life of the imagination.

In this same collection, *Discrepancies and Apparitions,* I introduce another mythic character who does not come from a dream, as Jennifer Snow does, but who is connected with dreams for me, and who evolved in the same way that Jennifer Snow did. This is the character of Daniel, who also was based on someone with whom I was briefly acquainted as an undergraduate at Berkeley. In my senior year, he won the same poetry contest that I had won when I was a junior. I think I was both attracted to his talent, the fact that he was very handsome and seemed sophisticated, and very fearful that my favorite professor, Tom Parkinson, would like him and his poems better than me. This fear of betrayal and replacement is the source of almost all my shadow life.

Somehow in my imagination, the way that image of Ann Yothers became Jennifer Snow, the image of Daniel Moore became the Daniel of my poems who is a kind of page of cups, another tarot card image. In my mind, the name Daniel is associated with lions, and in this poem Daniel has something to do with the way in which lions, an image of royalty for me, come into life and dignify it. In "Possession Poem," also from this collection, and even more a poem that becomes a catalogue of Wakoski images, named early in the poem as oranges, mirrors, birds, children, horses, metal, Daniel is a character represented as perhaps a younger rival for royalty:

> All right, Daniel,
> I'm tired of talking to you in symbols.
> Let us use plain language,
> hard facts.
> Let's get this out in the open,
> make it real.
> I was in this chair first.
> That means it was mine first.

While dreams have always been important to me and certainly have provided a powerful source of imagery and even narrative in my poems, I believe that during the early 1960s in New York, while I was actively writing out of dreams, I began to bypass the actual dream for a waking creation of dream images. That's the way I view my invention of *The George Washington Poems*. They came out of the same kind of process that in a dream makes you see yourself in somebody else's body. It's the way that in a dream you might see someone or something that you are intimate with transformed into the figure of someone or something else that is strange or unexpected. Thus, I become Jennifer Snow whom I can control, or someone in my life who has become a rival for what I perceive as my poetry success is transformed into Daniel whom I can also control, via the dreams and poems. It is an easy leap from this dream process to deciding that you will write poems/letters to a dead American mythic hero, George Washington, speaking to him as if he were the lover you live with, or the father who betrayed you, or another man whom you long for and/or idealize. This transformation gives you some control over your life, if only in the dreamworld or the fantasy world of the imagination.

I believe that once this leap was made, I had accomplished the process for creating a personal mythology. While I locate the source of my ideas for creating a personal mythology in another early poem, written while I was an undergraduate at Berkeley, "Justice Is Reason Enough," I clearly understand in retrospect that I had no idea what I was doing then. I wrote the poem out of psychological urgency, the need to tell my story, but was overwhelmed by my shame at telling a documentary version of my stories. So, I invented a story that I thought was beautiful, romantic, and could be co-opted for myself.

The story involved the creation of a twin brother, which of course is the animus of Diane Wakoski, and perhaps even a version of her shadow. This twin brother has to be so close, erotically close, that together they commit incest, and in the story told by the poem, the brother also has to commit suicide, kill himself for the shame of it. Or course, psychologically, this is Diane killing off the shadow half of herself, the animus, so that she can claim her wholeness, her anima, which is the source of her identity as a woman. Also as poet, I might add. However, in this poem I attribute this event to a dream, while paying a bit of a tribute to Yeats's "Second Coming" in doing so:

> Mother took me back there every day for
> over a year and asked me, in her whining way, why it had to happen
>
> over and over again—until I wanted
> never to hear of David any more. How
> could I tell her of his dream about the gull beating its wings
> effortlessly together until they drew blood?
>
> Would it explain anything, and how . . .

While I did not dream this experience, I did invent it in the same manner that dreams occur, to represent an actual event that happened, through one so different that no one could easily compare the two. Thus, are dreams devious and not necessarily easy to interpret, and I realized that poems could be that way too. In retrospect, I think that pointing to a dream being connected with the dramatic events in the poem, even offering it as an oblique explanation, was a prescient gesture on my part. I believe I must have known subconsciously that the dream process was not only connected with poetry, or provided a clue to the mystery of a poem, but also that the dream itself was a kind of icon to be introduced into a poem, like the door in the children's closet that lets them through to the land of Narnia.

Once I discovered some of the secrets of creating a personal mythology via understanding a bit about the dream process itself, I never really had to depend on dreams themselves again as a source of my poems. Which is not to say that I don't willingly use them, whenever they offer themselves. But it's almost as if my waking imagination is a better dreamer now than my unconscious. However, dreams themselves will always be springboards for my poetry, though I suspect that never again in my life will I be gifted with anything like those serial dreams I had so many years ago, where my life went on in movie-star brilliance, fairy-tale excitement, always with the floors covered with bolts of green silk cloth.

JANE O. WAYNE

Jane Wayne's first collection, *Looking Both Ways*, was selected by David Wagoner for the 1984 Devins Award. Her second volume of poetry, *A Strange Heart*, was selected by James Tate as the winner of the 1996 Marianne Moore Poetry Prize. It also received the Society of Midland Authors Poetry Award. Wayne has taught creative writing at Washington University and Webster University in St. Louis, where she lives.

ONE HAND ON THE PEN, ONE IN THE DREAM

J ust as a monk in lotus position doesn't will enlightenment or a dreamer doesn't will a dream—a poet doesn't will a poem.

A woman once told me that her small son would dangle his fishing rod off the end of his bed by the hour. He must have been a poet: Fishing in the air. Waiting for that sudden tug. That flash of excitement. Something out of nothing.

I wish I could say that sitting down to write, I have rituals, foolproof tricks—some key that opens the door to poetry. I haven't. That boy understood how we cast our lines and wait for inspiration to bite. Sometimes I start with a blank page or screen and let words flow, until something snags my attention. A spider on a houseplant, a bowl of lumpy porridge, a zipper catching on a loose thread. Once I feel that pull, no matter how unlikely the image, I examine it, unwrapping it, like some shiny-ribboned box, until it reveals its secret, until the thread and zipper, for example, turn into a line about forgetting: "Mid-thought she stops / the way a zipper catches on a loose thread." The personal pull an image exerts must come from the unconscious—some part of me that knows before I do and more than I do.

At my desk, when a word or image won't come, I often hear the old formula for free association: *Follow your thoughts.* Court the loose logic of your dreams. Sometimes in the less-than-lucid interval before I fall asleep, my mind turns to, and even solves, the day's poetic problem— say a missing beat or an unresolved ending. More often in this dreamy state, my mind spills out, gurgling on its own, like an overturned jug. If I try to catch it on the page, it evaporates. At most, I might retrieve a few drops that memory soaked up overnight.

I've also learned to look for unexpected visits—"the subjective recollections" that Proust describes. If I'm alert, the whole scene, such as my mother playing the piano next to me, returns in detail. Then before the poetic impulse gets into words, whatever it is that floats between the page and the mind—the keyboard of a piano, the sound of an arpeggio, her hands lowering the fallboard—takes on a dreamlike presence. The whole time I'm writing about that green-walled living room, I'm seated in it—legs dangling from the wooden piano bench again. No wonder that after a whole day of writing, if asked about the piece in progress, I often go blank—the way waking, one forgets a dream.

The following poem arose out of an actual dream in which biting down, I felt my tooth crumble.

Tooth and Nail

> "Every tooth in a man's head is
> worth more than a diamond."
> *Miguel Cervantes*

Last night my necklace broke.
Bending in a dream, I heard silk tear at the seams.
I filled my palm with pearls, all knobby and yellow.

Now as I bite this thread in two,
the spool jumps off my lap.
One palm stays in the dream, one on my skirt.

Slowly turned, its blue veins rise.
The skin sits loosely on its back, like this old sweater.
I grow a size too small for myself.

Nothing fits.
Not even this shelf in the pantry.
Lately I have to stand on my toes to reach it.

I save my voice, but this single-minded tongue
keeps circling over my losses.
I count the teeth marks in my apple and make do.

Maybe tonight you will come like a lost word
or a coin under my pillow.
I watch my fingernails return.

Only a month after dreaming that my tooth crumbled, the dentist told me I had, in fact, a hairline fissure in a molar! Though the mysterious interweaving of dream and reality generated the poem, the crumbling-tooth dream itself was discarded along the way. Instead, the poem's dream derives from an actual mishap—the ripping of an antique dress, which becomes: "Bending in a dream, I heard silk tear at the seams." The next line, those pearls turning to teeth, "all knobby and yellow" in my palm, was purely imagined, the sort of transformation that might happen in a dream. In the next stanza, as the poem's speaker bites the thread, the dream haunts her. And dreams do haunt us, even at our desks.

How different, then, the writing of the dream is from dreaming. I spend countless hours revising a poem—fiddling endlessly with syntax, turning lines this way and that, chanting under my breath until every word is right, every phrase is in the right place. I try to console myself with Yeats's melodic lines:

> I said, "A line will take us hours maybe;
> Yet if it does not seem a moment's thought
> Our stitching and unstitching has been naught."

No doubt, this phase of writing also bows to some aesthetic faculty we're scarcely conscious of—call it instinct, intuition, the unconscious—but, on the whole, revising entails reasoning or critical thinking—an analytical process we rarely observe at work in our effortless dreams.

The compression of the following dream astounded me. It found its way into a poem about grief which starts with these lines:

> After he died,
> I dreamed that the phone rang
> and when I said "hello",
> his slow throaty voice rising slightly,
> holding on to that last syllable
> said "good bye"—

How could my waking mind match that dream in all its brevity!

For a writer, dreams are a source of inspiration, or as Proust puts it in *The Past Recaptured*: "I reflected that dreams would sometimes in their way bring nearer to me truths or impressions which would not come through my own unaided effort . . . . I would not scorn this second muse, this nocturnal muse." A good resolve for poets, too.

My thirteen-year-old daughter had a recurring dream which resonated for me, as if I had dreamed it myself. The unstoppable car seemed archetypal—some version of the body, some rage or passion that's uncontrollable. But how could a car, a modern invention, be an archetype? That question prodded me into the poem:

Your Recurring Dream

Haven't you noticed
there's often something you can't put away
before you fall asleep
like a necklace that won't unfasten
or pull over your head—something left undone
that nags at you—a white slip of a thought
half-hanging out of a closed drawer?
You dream the way you hold your blue jeans
upside down, shaking them to get
the day's loose change out of the pockets.

If you had nightmares in the last century,
you might have awakened tugging the reins
of some runaway in an open field—
instead of clutching the steering wheel
of your downhill dream—
always speeding, always pushing the brakes
through the floor of consciousness,
night after night, belted
into the same driver's seat,
locked into a dream that never crashes.

In the first drafts, the poem started with the car image. At some point, I daydreamed myself into her bedroom, and things came alive. The necklace, the white slip, the blue jeans—they all related to the subject at hand. I also used some Freudian lore rattling in my head, the notion that dream material derives from the day's thoughts or events; so she's shaking blue jeans *to get the day's loose change out of the pockets*. The poem itself took a lot of shaking to get the pieces to fall into place. In the end, I realized that a recurring dream, almost by definition, cannot be resolved, so I reordered the stanzas to emphasize the tension of the last five lines. Poems, like dreams, begin and end in mystery. They both raise unanswerable questions.

This itself is what attracts me to writing poetry, not the knowable but the unknowable—and the way a mind can, at the strangest times, surprise itself, the way a dream does. What else compares to the thrill of our lone thoughts turning a corner we didn't know was there? Why else write poetry—or fish in air?

THEODORE WEISS

LAYLE SILBERT

Since 1943 Theodore Weiss, with his wife,
Renée, has edited the highly influential *Quarterly
Review of Literature;* but it is primarily as a poet
that he is known. From *The Catch* (1951) to
Selected Poems (1995) and beyond, more than a
dozen volumes have captured his passionate wit.
He has also published several books of criticism,
including *The Breath of Clowns and Kings: A Study
of Shakespeare* (1971). The 1997 recipient of the
Williams/Derwood Award for poetry, Weiss
taught for many years at Bard College before
moving to Princeton, where he is currently writ-

ing collaborative poems with Renée. Poems of
theirs have appeared in the *Nation*, the *New
Republic*, *American Poetry Review*, and other periodicals. Recently PEN honored them with a Lifetime Achievement Award for editing *QRL*.

REMEMBERING "CALIBAN REMEMBERS"

Poetry and dreams, their similarity and their impact on each other? For prime intelligence on this subject it is hard to think of a better source than the master dreamer and dream master, Shakespeare. He employed dreams in each of the major genres of drama and with the particular efficacy each genre required.

For the choicest dream work one must turn to *The Tempest*. Here dreams and poetry overlap, if they do not become one. From the start, we, like most of the cast, are taken in by Prospero's magical art, the dream-vivid tempest he produces. And then within the play we encounter dreams, high and low, to be followed in the end by Prospero's cloud-capping speech which acknowledges the reality of dreams, as well as the dream nature of so-called reality.

For years that now seem at least as long as my life, I have been charmed by *The Tempest*. With every reading its spell has grown stronger. And it has become an ultimate statement for me of the magical nature of things: the last, best proof that, with pathos or feeling potential everywhere, the pathetic fallacy is not altogether fallacious. Above all, through a kin sympathy for Caliban, my thoughts and feelings collected around him. A character who could speak as he did—

> Sometimes a thousand twangling instruments
> Will hum about mine ears; and sometime voices,
> That, if I then had wak'd after long sleep,
> Will make me sleep again; and then, in dreaming,
> The clouds methought would open, and show riches
> Ready to drop upon me; that, when I wak'd,
> I cried to dream again—

surely exceeded Prospero's fierce denunciation. Such speech persuaded me that Prospero had failed—if Shakespeare had not—to understand the true nature of Caliban and to treat him as he needed and deserved to be treated.

Indeed, beyond his expressiveness, Caliban's descendentalism, his absorption in the delicious minute particulars of nature, he a kind of shaggy pre-imagist, wholly won me. As did his complicated relationship with Prospero and Miranda, one, as I saw it, made up of equal parts of hate and love. Thus increasingly Caliban attracted me as a character perfect in his person and his circumstances for a dramatic monologue. Perfect also at embodying our human condition, our earthbound yet haunted estrangement; taught speech, what, except for inspired moments like Caliban's above, has our communicating, with nature or with our fellows, come to? What have we done with language but, cursing, abused it, denied it and ourselves? Notwithstanding Browning's brilliant if idiosyncratic treatment in "Caliban on Setebos," Auden's odd, customarily perverse portrait in "The Sea and the Mirror," and other explorations of Caliban, I felt certain that he remained a multidimensional treasure trove waiting to be unearthed.

But a basic dilemma presented itself. The rowdy pair, Trinculo and Stephano, had spoken of what sport it would be, and more importantly what profit, to take Caliban back with them to Naples as a sideshow. However, exposed and rebuked as they are, they are hardly in any position to carry out their fantasies. And though Prospero claims

Caliban as his own, he—or Shakespeare—says nothing of Caliban's disposal once Prospero and the others leave the island. Is Caliban taken or forsaken? In short, Shakespeare—whether by oversight or by insight (a creature like Caliban, wild if partly tamed, lost between beast and human, what future could it expect among so-called civilized men?)—considerately enough left both options open.

Long and hard I pondered the two possibilities; for the obvious, if different, benefits derivable from both, the two versions seemed just about equally appealing. But, captivated by the isle's natural and magical delights, as well as by the advantages supplied by unity of place and time, I cast my poem's lot with Caliban's being left behind. One could ascribe it either to the commotion inevitably attending the ship's hectics at departure or to Caliban's panic, his hiding away in some fastness of the island for fear of the bobbing, sail-crackling ship and the treacherous sea, and also of forsaking the only home he knew. Fear especially after encountering several new representatives of the world he would be going to. Obnoxious as those examples proved to be, would they not counterweigh whatever entanglements Caliban had with Prospero and Miranda?

And there Caliban was, except for his fantastic memories, alone on his island, left to try to understand what had happened. Had Prospero and Miranda and then the troublesome strangers really materialized or was it all a preposterous show, a low jinks, an intricate dream staged by Setebos to put Caliban to excruciating torments? Torments poignant far beyond the island's extremest nips and pinches; let Caliban toss on the rack of his own rampant imagination as tantalizing riches indeed poured out of the heavens of his thoughts.

So my poem proceeded. And as it became ever more engrossing, not only devouring my days, but stealing into my sleep as well, more and more I fitted into Caliban's hairy, horny, yet ultrasensitive skin. Thus one late night, when the fever and exhilaration of the unfolding poem was exceptionally strong, I had a most prodigious dream—Caliban's I hasten to say, not Bottom's, but perhaps they are not so different after all? I was in the middle of the other option. And exultantly I lived it: the ship's tumultuous passage, the briny heave of the waves, a landlubber's seasickness in stormy hours, his abuse by the sailors, and his near death. And, finally, the arrival at that stinking, brawling city, Naples by name. Actually another island, England, but how antipodal to Caliban's: a terrifying jungle of jangling noises, snarling people, creatures, and infernal devices they called machines waiting to devour one. Were these the cloud-capped towers Prospero had described, merely one more riches-battering dream or, rather, an overwhelming nightmare?

And then the heart-rending moments of meetings. Especially that one when I-Caliban, going through my paces as an entertainment in a sideshow, see entering the tent a lovely woman and a delicate yet vivacious child. My heart leaped as though it must break out of my body. "Miranda!" fairly flew to my lips. But she, after the shadow of a frown and a moment's puzzled look, smiling, joined in her child's amusement. And I locked my cry away. For how could I let her know that this outlandish "it," face smeared with paints, in gaudy-colored, multilayered, stinking rags, crawling and scampering as the stage-master bid, was Caliban?

Finally—most overpowering of all—the explosion of a long-brewing plot in which Prospero and Miranda are imprisoned by their enemies, planning their death, and I am called upon—as I call upon Ariel and the other elements—to save them. With the last moment Lear-ish enough, as Prospero, seeing me, dies on the dagger-point of recognition! Having such extremities in sight, is it any wonder I chose the other course?

I woke, the crackling atmosphere of my dream's electricity still much upon me. For it had been as though I had lived, however briefly, in the very real, local circumstances of an Elizabethan episode. Or at least at the center of a rehearsal or performance of one of Shakespeare's plays as he himself was putting it on. Once or twice in the past, during a moment of absorption in a class occupied with a Shakespearean play, for a moment indeed, the curtains parted and unheard-of riches—the actual, contingent Elizabethan world, its sizzling, beehive hubbub—stormed around me. The sting was there, and the heavenly nectar. For a moment. Then the curtains clapped shut.

And except for an after-tingle and flitting, quickly fading shadows, little of my dream was left. The question of moment is what bearing did that dream, however powerful and luxuriant it may have been, have upon the poem I wrote. Still I am confident that, like the numerous cities of Troy, each one built out of and buried in the others, my dream sent shoots of energy through the final version, ensured it a resonance—a life behind its life—the poem would otherwise have lacked.

The whole matter of dreams and of the extent of their impact on one's writing is, of course, a fascinating but elusive one. I usually dream very little, at least consciously. The explanation for this which I have, if tentatively, arrived at is that, in a busy writing life, I, through insistent poems, usually claiming my dreams, consume them before they can reach my sleep. But perhaps, more honestly, for my dreams' very repetitiousness, I scarcely apprehend them.

However, I do know that sometimes when I have set a fairly ambitious poem a-sail, most of all when I have lived with it a good while, as with the Caliban, the poem invades my sleep. And in that luxurious stage between sleep and wake, with only a thin cover of sleep upon me, my nose sticking out, something fundamental that I had been groping toward comes clear or the poem, a snag in it untied, takes a sudden, urgent surge forward. In such semi-sleep the mind and its powers are free, without distractions outside or in, to exult in themselves to the full. Cleaving through doubts and other obstacles, the mind enjoys its magnificent magic realism and a cogent logic all its own. At these blessed moments the poem in its making feeds the dream even as the dream feeds the poem, a seemingly boundless rain of riches.

Caliban Remembers

I

       Might
have gone with them. Might. To be—
I heard their scheming—a strange fish,
seasick on land, lurching in shadows,
a monster then, tormenting, make.
No one for me. Not my master's kind
with perfumes stinking, auks at courting.
Nor to me true friends those two
I fell in with.
       Oh fell in with,
a horse-pond for our pains, and over
ears, scum sticking to, thick scum.

"Putrid fish," all jeered at me.
As if, from king on down, they did
not take their fishy turn in the sea.
As in the way they reached this shore.

On such a day—moons marching by
my marking time—sat I out here,
sat, shading me, beneath this cliff.
The sea, one blinding wave, bulged round.
The sun had soaked deep into it,
into each bush, each tree. Had soaked
into these rocks until they shook
with light.
       There—I fished then too—
a great wind suddenly blowing up,
foam in its mouth, a bloody shriek,
that boat.
       Again and again surf broke
on it. Yet sparkling everywhere,
a blaze that, sizzling, blazed the more,
boat, gliding over this cove's jag rocks,
rode in.
       By then, for lightning's rifts,
one wave hot after me the sea,

I scuttled off, got me to
my cave's dark cleft and, glad at last
to have it, hid.
                My rod dangles,
once more sways the waters, swelling
from the line. New shadows risen,
noises I hear past what such brooding
high-noon brings. Hummings out of the sea
and the air, out of the woods?
                                Long tides
ago, I remember, hardly remember,
there were others. Low voices, rough,
could find me out, prod me, please.
No wasp's bite sharper, whirring through,
no grape-burst sweeter. Vague at best
now, like that name he'd knot to me.

Yet things I have belonged to them.
This gown, a giant ringdove's rainbow-
downy hood, I lounge in, tatters
and all, once my master at his magic
needs must wear, with his rod fishing
outlandish cries, their creatures in them,
from air and sea.
                    Lurked among books
he left. At times, efts in heaped leaves,
as out of sleep, they pop. Yet as I
bend they fade, day after day,
farther away.
                But next to my hand
this pebble, blinked at me, a trinket
it might have been, dropped that time
I stumbled on her dreaming here,
dazzled by her still, as her glass,
cast off, raised to the face, a look
flashing, says she's, passing, teasing,
by behind me.
                Chalk-faced, hair
sleeked down, no otter better, stalked

behind her, basking in her light,
so darking me who saw her first,
that Ferdinand.
                    How push back
this crinkle badgers brow?
                         Witch she,
not my poor mother, I tweaked as ever,
as a jay its secretest feather.
And most, blood at the heart hopping,
dare I speak out her name.
                              Sometimes
taste still—remembering bubbles—gust
of that liquor. Cloud-casked surely,
music fermented. Those two bidding me
drink, one gulp, and no more goading
for me. God I, the sky my gliding,
earth, everything in it my subject,
far below.
            Now, if ever they were,
gone. Even my sleep, only rarely
whispering in it, slips free of them.

From the thicket, peeping, watched
the long ship I helped stow fruit, fish,
water aboard sweep out and silently,
its sails confused with clouds, folding,
unfolding, melt as though the wind,
seeing them go, blew merrily.

At first I also, kicking up heels,
scattered round their garments, linens,
books. At first. But after—how find
again that whole belonging mine
before they came?—and worst those days
when I, a smoke, fume through my hands,
loneliness whelms me.

Had I only
his book's good company, that company
it kept waiting, perfect, on him,
humble the world, I'd lord it truly.

My rod, sprouting though it did
from the staff he thought forever buried
and I plucked it, swish as it will
to rouse the breezes, rustle the sea,
fares forth no revelries like his,
nor no revelations neither.

Times I'd welcome the old, heavy
chores, his orders at roughest irk,
echoed in cramps, nips, pinches,
hedgehogs packed and inchmeal wedging
through me.
                    Times they rack me still,
those pokes, side-stitches (feared at first—
my shivers mounted—he'd returned;
aches he had, all kinds, fit
for each part of the body, aches
he must have stuffed in hollow branches
sealed with pitch, then like the noises
from his pipe, at will puffed out);
and shapes they do inside the dark,
torching me that I slubber in bogs,
on mad bushes burr me, furzes clawing.
But now not meant for me, no ape-
mouthing sprites behind them to mock,
not anger, only themselves.
                                Themselves
those plumes awag at the water's edge,
draggled through mire, flood, yet dry,
a play straight out of the spume?

                                              Not those
from the ship again, untouched, a miracle,
unless the shine they sport be sea's
(my master bragged he kept them so),
but tailing one another, great bugs.

Well, whatever comes pleases me,
my state on the isle. Its flocks and herds,
its slyest creatures, these, as I pluck
for hides, food, feathers, tribute
also in their squawky cowering,
scrape to me King. Tame too
as they never were for those. Long days
I loll, ruler and subjects the same.

Even so things I learned, some,
nag at me still, names that, shimmering,
as I would clamp jaws to, dissolve.
And the faces glimmered out at me
from bush and sky, tide-riding shapes.

Came on her in this very cove,
swimming still on her, whiter, rounder
than a wave, open to the sun.
Then I understood his daily command:
"Stand upright, stand!" Upright I was,
knew at last what he meant by "Be
a man." Saw she was gone there, torn
out by the roots. Wish in sudden,
flushed kindness, pity, give her mine,
all.
      But tiptoed, manhood in hand,
to surprise her, completed while she slept,
as by magic—was it our fires,
crossing, drew him?—scepter quivering,
upright, he appears. Eyes blazed
on me, cares, it seems, nothing
I have learned my lesson, quick
to obey.

Fear he had I'd fish
his pond? Oh no, not fish it, stock it!
Who else was there to do her turn,
so save the day for the likes of me,
and him as well, on the island?

Not all his magic, age, can angle
new foundlings, me more, out of air.
Even now loss wrings me.
                              Still his words,
crackling, strike me everywhere stony,
yet shaking too. One frown farther
I had been done.

II
                              But hear that hiss.
A rumbling scrabble, skin atwitch,
the sea would speak?
                              Lo! The rod
grows taut, throbs, humming, in my hands.

There, dripping, spluttering thick sighs,
bobs a swollen, slippery thing.
Some odd, mad fish I've caught!

Clutch it.
          A book!
                    Alive again:
inside its blotched pages, seasick,
for all the sights, blood-chilling worlds,
it's gulped, words, through fingers slither-
ing minnows, hop.
                    Mixed in its spells now,
nymphs once cropped, nymphs and urchins,
romping, couple, splotched purple swirling.

Clouds my master called this world,
clouds and dreams (a sorcerer then,
a stronger, over him, mouthing things,
wording us, thus puffed into being,
browsing on our aches and rages?)

Such waking cloud this book's become.
Reading before, its gnat-words fidgety,
not hard enough!
                Yet some, tails flouncing
as if plunged into the sea, beswamped
by smudgy ink, I know again.

Put ear to page. Hear something.
Grumbling steady, far off collecting.
His voice, is it, penned in the words?

That voice—like it no other sound—
which, first stroking, then grown gruff,
kept its kindness for this book
he turned to more and more, the rough
of it all that was left and there
to abuse me.
              Master he may have been,
yet could do nothing without me. Not,
unless I, fetching sticks, patched fire,
rouse his magic, its high-flown tricks.
Whatever his flights, had to return
to this island, his cell, me.
Never could, whatever his flights,
go back to his country till they came
with that ship.
              I alone propped him, kept
as earth does sky, else dropped in the sea.

Why then should I not use it also?
Shake me out music, that brave host,
showering praises, presents isle-heaped:
luscious fruits flung from the trees;
liquors clouds, cask-big, split,
pour down, thirsty for my tongue;
fish pied flying in out of waves
as the sea itself, glistening, bows,
then at my feet stows dutiful ships,
with treasure crammed as palm-tall hives,
their honeycombs oozing.

Maybe can,
why not, raise one fair as she,
a dozen, sea-blooms, wreathing her,
bent on one thing only, hooked,
dolphin-sleek, dished in the sun,
one thing: pleasing me.
Cloudy as sky,
bow-taut, is growing, better begin.
Drape the robes about me, so.
Wagging the staff, half crouch, half stiff,
nose raised as if snuffling scents,
the music working under things.

Now find the place in the book.
Here,
the lines most faded. Head nodding
right, then left, both eyes rolling,
till body drops away.
(Never knew
I spied on him mumbo-jumboing,
then jutting ear as if he thought
to hear answer. Was there something,
mutters, say the air's bright crest,
aflutter, speaking, speaking I
now seem to be hearing out of these
drowsy trees?)
Oh, could he see
me now, his lessons like his scepter
clutched, the earth, the sea, the cloud-
packed sky about to wake, how pleased
he'd have to be.
I can, mouth plumped,
almost repeat that rounded phrase
finished off in a hiss.
Lo, now, lo!
Even as I say it, darkness hedges,
crowding out of the sea.

Beware!
A lightning crashes, fire's scribble
scratchy down sky; and that oak, sky-high,
falls at my feet.
                    One twig closer
and I had been—homage truly!—ever
crowned.
                    Wake that squall again?
Watching him manage it, hearing
out of it bellows, no beasts madder,
demons not (suppose more loosed
than he could handle?), shuddered me
through.
                    There, high on squall's ruff,
an osprey its spray, a cormorant beaking,
in the distance riding, gay as a porpoise,
the ship bobs that took them off!

Desire that: my master back,
she, the others, firewood, fast rooted
where I dumped it, ache in my bones,
the play—I ever cast for monster,
slave, with real blows in it, hurting
words—to be played over and over?

Oh no. Now that his book's mine,
my lackeys they.
                    Ah the sweet tasks
I would conjure for them as—standing,
upright, rigid, by, they glare,
if cast down, deadly looks—I lie
in my flower-puffed bed, she, flower
among flowers, by me, mistress
to my least worded, far fetched whim.

And him I bid bring turtle eggs,
struggle through fanged briers for berries,
prickles too of bees he must snatch
choicest honeysacks from.

                    The others,
husked of rapiers, ruffs, fine airs,
down on all fours, the beasts they are,
cuff them, kick. Out of their yelping,
as master's pipe could ply a storm,
pluck music.
                    One bears me a bowl
brims rose water, petals swimming;
and dabbling hands, on another I wipe.
Then order these pour the good wine
down throat. Or "Scratch the regal back
with porcupine." Wanting the palace
his book shows, "Scoop out that fen.
Put rocks over there. There. And there."
And, put, not liking it, "Put back
again."
                    But as they, drooping, sigh,
their struts and frets, wildfire plots,
gone out, would I not let them be,
him most, most haggard for these labors
far beyond his years, and he, first,
landing on this shore, enjoying
for a time what he found here, most kind?
As I enjoyed, a time, the silks,
the warmth, the tunes he (she more) soothed
against me.
                    Best in that moment when,
as now, shadows deepen the wood.
Then, he piping, I sprawled by,
the notes bubbling, moonlight dewy
on them, as in her eyes, already
gleaming secrets of caves, sea-kept,
she sang. And winds and waves, chins set
in their hands, the stars, leant down, peering
ever harder as darkness ripened,
also sang. One radiant sound,
the earth and sky involved in it,
soaked into me, I shook with light.

So he, sitting over me, listened,
I at fishing not more still.
Points at things, making fish mouths,
stranger noises. And a mote
baiting my eye, a mayfly twirling,
whole day, if tiny, on midnoon,
prods with "Mind, mind!" till at last,
no salmon swifter thrashing waters,
flipped above the spray, the word,
words loosed, stream from my mouth.
Joy in him then, love like my own.
Eager to show me this thing, that.
His books spread out before me, shared,
I learn to pin their swart bugs down.

A book, it seems, for everything,
for things that cannot be and never
could. Had one even showing me
and in it called "Caliban"
because I fed, not less gladly
than on ants, on men. How could I,
no man being here? And think
of eating those, washed up, rotten,
worse than flotsam, on this shore!
To them alone such name belongs
who would, not cold, not hungry, kill.
(The name I had I never told,
with mother buried who gave it me.)

But best of all that warbling book,
as on a cloud inscribed, about clouds.
The world so graved, growing, changes,
one thing into another, like a cloud,
its women turning, as the pages
do, into a tree, a brook,
a song. Who would have thought their looks,
their voices, now only a windy leaf,
a rivulet, the hearer's tears
start forth, the world seen newly
in their light.

But am not I,
not merely stone, such changeling too?
So she, in one day sped from childhood
stalk-thin, gawky, into woman.
What I became she could not see
but only heard, as I would sigh,
the same old shaggy husk of me,
as that god, changed, so the book said,
into a bull for love, must bellow.

His books I browsed on. All but one.
No matter how I yearned, heaven
it loomed, mocking over my head.
And that the book I saw him lost
in, sitting by the fire, listening
to its gossip, mingled with the jiggly
words, his stare outglaring embers.
That tongue, so good at wagging, flogging,
little about him then but as it
jogs off on its own. And the eye
that easily caught me out, no eye
for me, a thing that never was.

Mornings too, quick to me earth,
the berries restless in their plot,
the sky as well, I knew it time
to tend the day. But he shut away
as though, beyond those pages marked,
no light, no joy, can bloom.
                              Damned be
such book when world in lark enough,
in filbert and in plum, cries out
that I become a winged hearing,
lapping tongue, and those the ground-
work eyes and hands abound them in,
my feelings, ripened as they ripe.

Let him be buried in his glimmering
dark while I sprawl in the sun,
in busy, slow pleasure running hot
fingers over me. Or, plunging,
lounge inside the thicket, tickled
by the shade, webs buzzing, leaf-mold
rotting on mold, a wood-bug sometimes
gulped with a berry.
             Long hours on
and into the night within my fingers,
under my lids, the daylight tingles,
tingle too along my dreams
those sozzled smells, the fruits as when
I munched on them.
             And he, after,
the fire gone out? Grey, ash-grey.

Yet that one book, even as I have it,
is it better than the world, telling
where winds are woven, snows, sundowns,
showing them being made, and played
out as its owner bids?
             Some god
must have bestowed it on my master,
else dropped it—as later he did—
lying open, wind-leafed, wind-sighing,
like this earth, and my master found it.

Time and place forgot, he wandered
in it, blissfully bound by soundings
he could make.
             So on this island
all seasons at once or, as he wished,
seasons from strange countries,
mountains in his cell and light
as clouds, tall mountains flaming round
the embers, goddesses too and sprites—
the rites of them.

But then he saw—
perhaps the days between the spells,
their willingness to work, grew longer,
harder, or he woke, ash-grey—
what empty dream he'd snared him in,
learned the lesson I had always known:
with that book to give himself, to dive
into the thrilling waters, chilled
at times, hard buffeting, this world,
this life is?
        No, angrier he grew,
his words mocking him. Angrier,
words like blows.
           Never knew,
I, finding words he did not know,
like new, hidden nests could show him,
eggs speckled with writing brighter
than his book's, sly birds, the topmost
sky still breathing from their wings,
in their songs still.
          Then he might
have, once more trusting me, entrusted
the isle, as mate his daughter.
              Instead
that feathery, ribboned thing! May he,
filched my place with the logs, her fancy
also, drown this time for good,
a delicate food lining fish bellies,
sweet between my royal teeth
(Caliban called, Caliban be).
Then, who knows, she might, seeing
him at last so much in me,
me like the more.

Or, better, let him,
soaked enough, grown scaly through
and through, yanked out, Caliban me.
If he, pale sprout, could supplant me,
why I not him? Three times as much
as his dragged, staggering, poor armful,
he a king's son, I can haul.

Our names with their three syllables,
two mountains humping a crouched "i"—
Cal-i-ban and Ferd-i-nand,
Ferdinand and Caliban
(somewhere in between Miranda)—
like enough so that the mouth
which shaped out his with loving breath,
a trill the birds would stop to hear,
to mine could be as kissing-kind?
Ah, well, would she ever have—
how could she—loved a thing like me?

Why, instead of all that work,
those lessons, slow, dull, scratchy,
did my master, worlds at hand,
not turn me presto into prince?
Sea, fire, sky he managed
featly; but I too much for him,
an earth magic alone could never change?

Never, as he sought to stuff me
with his learning, asked he me
my thought, my feeling. All I was
was wrong, to change. All he wished
was aping, my face wrought to look,
a mirror, more and more like his.

III

The book in hand, past teaching now.
Try the last words.

                        That grating stink!
Up it dredges from grottos, bogs,
sunk under the sea.

                        And swelling out,
choking the air, one racketing cry.

He's back, overseeing me, making me
do what I do? Or Setebos
with his accursed crew, sneaked in
at last and most to devil me—
who else is left to feed their hate?—
for being driven off?

                        A crack
as though the earth is splitting!

                                    Out there,
lit, the ocean spouts. One monstrous
fish?

            No, upright, like a mighty
man in flashing robes and roars—
would I could give this book to him!—
I see it, see his city, so he
called it, climbing the skies, its spires,
cloud-piled, the gardens multiplied
with gilded fountains, songs torch-lit,
and women, each a little bower,
while far below dark fires rage,
the swamp on which such city's built.

Like torrents crashing over a crag,
aimed, writing its zigzag, a lightning
dashes over me.

Now crumbles,
tumbling, drags the outermost rim
of the isle with it!
                    My doing? Have done
no lone thing yet brings me one crumb
of joy; no singing—only this howling,
sky clipt open, trolls my name.

What if, the salt marsh flushed and pounced
on me, I move the moon, the sea
rushed over the isle, I among mollusks
down there, for sharks a crunchy music?

Ass enough that time I dreamed
I could, with those two clumsy sots,
set me free, be king. Master
I called one, god, licking his foot,
and he, for all the sack in him,
not mire good enough to cake
my master's boot. And I believed
he'd bottled moonshine, music, himself,
the moon's own man, dropped with them!

Oh lessoned I am. Off with the gown.
Break the wand. Before this book,
more than ever my master did,
rules over me, ruins entirely,
drown it again. Never wanted it
in the first place.
                    So let it sink.
Dissolved into the restlessly paging
(seems to be reading it), gurgling sea,
the nymphs and dolphins schooled by it,
it may, sea-changed, sigh out its message.
As now.
                    Whatever his tempest brought
about, this one washes me clean
of them, blundering on their tottery
two feet (upright they pride themselves
on being!), in broad daylight bethicketed,

wilder than night. And all the time
plotting.
    Then why so foolish
as to toss his power away and, naked,
return to a world bustling with men,
his brother, my silly crew, repeated
a thousand, thousand times over? Expose,
as well as himself, his dear daughter
to infections, plagues, far past the work
of scummy ponds!
      Devils they said
haunting this island. No least devil
till they arrived. Not all the toads
and frogs this island spawns could quell
the viper in them. Devils he sailed
away with, devils, waiting, hordes,
to dog him all his life's last days.
Think of a world, an island like this,
swarmed with them, their schemings, brawls!

Winds blow over me, the crooning
night air, free now, full of nothing
but its own breath, serenades
the locusts chirr, scents of the sea
and this my island, twining with
what stars are pouring.
     Yet, not burrs
snarled tighter in the hair, they cling,
that manyed voice, as in a sea-
shell, ebbing, wailing, far inside
into my ear.
    Fingers remember
the bowl they brought, his hand on it,
hers, the water gushed forth, sparkling,
laughter, worlds. I polishing,
how it gleamed out pleasure, over-
wrought with my face, fitting in
beside hers, his.

Its carvings music
swelling to the eye, the finger,
from the pipe the piper on it
raises who is blowing out
the rounded, cloud-big, smoky sky,
I enter it, the little landscape
centered in thick trees a wind
in fragrant waves is wreathing, wreathing
me, shapes watching.
                   Him I see,
see her approaching. Eyes smart,
fingers tingle, taught sly snaggings
of silk, as eyes are caught by her
skirt rustling, the drop of her lids
a deafening tide in the blood till I,
battered as by that liquor's gust,
for the flooding over me drown.

Oh no, not that again, not me
gone in the dark of too much light.
Not bowls, nor touching words, to push
me out of me.
               There, smash bowl
to the earth, the dust it after all
is. And through its shattered pieces,
him and her, those others scattered,
I tramp free, free as the air.

Not lost, all ebbed away as water,
precious wines words keep as casks,
for that he would have taught?
                   Too high,
he rose, reached past earth, while I
slumped, an earth, below.
               At last
as he gave up me, gave up spells,
mind changed, chose man, the life
that all men lead, a magic, dream
more than enough?

Preferred the bowl
as much at breaking, robes faded
and faces, dyings, their plots too,
their hates.
  And most that momentary,
everlasting human touch—to touch
Miranda's hand again! A queen now,
joy of children throning her
as they, shrill, ruckle round her knees?
And he, does he live still, sometimes,
head shaking, bent in some forgotten
corner over an old book,
muttering maybe "Caliban"?—
the fearful, wide-open risk of it,
touch that runs like lightning through,
feeling, as men feel, as men call it
real.
  No matter how I squat,
leaves thick and dark mixing, dark
from inside owl wings, bat's screechy
darting, my cave sealed off, I stick out,
prickly, listening.
  How I long
to hear once more those me-completing
voices. Come back, would cast me
at their feet. And yet . . . alone, alone
as he must be, loathing, pitying, loving.

RICHARD WILBUR

CONSTANCE STUART LARRABEE

Richard Wilbur has served as poet laureate of the United States, and his many other honors include the National Book Award, two Pulitzer Prizes, and the Bollingen Translation Prize. He is a member of the American Academy of Arts and Letters, the American Academy of Arts and Sciences, and the Academy of American Poets. His numerous works include *New and Collected Poems* (1987) and translations of the plays of Molière and Racine. The essay that follows was written in response to an inquiry from the magazine *Dreamworks* and was reprinted (in different form) in Wilbur's collection *The Catbird's Song: Prose Pieces, 1963–1995*. Mr. Wilbur divides his time between Key West and Cummington, Massachusetts.

A NOTE ON POETRY AND DREAMS

The "dream aesthetics" in my work would be most obvious in such a poem as "Walking to Sleep," which derives from a sort of exploratory dreaming which I experience (and some others, apparently, do not), or in the later poem "In Limbo," which has to do with the conversing of all one's selves and ages in the hypnopompic state. But even where dreaming is not the subject, I know that the drifting, linking, and swerving of my poetry is often modeled—even while I strive for a conscious clarity and point—on the flow of consciousness in dream. I also know that it was my own experience as a dreamer which first led me—reading a paperback in a foxhole at Monte Cassino—to sense a submerged pattern of psychic action in the fiction of Poe, about whom I have since written a number of interpretive essays.

You ask for "a dream," and I am not sure whether to give you one which I understand or one which I do not. When I was sixteen, I dreamt of the appearance of an equestrian figure—a cowboy, I think—on the road which led past the gate of the walled vegetable garden and rounded the manure-house behind the barn. The figure gestured to the pine grove across the garden, and to a range of hazy blue mountains, Rockies-like, which had never appeared behind the pine grove before. In a deep, oracular voice, which seemed to be speaking close to my ear, the rider said, "Those are the Old Catica Mountains." I woke up with a feeling of awe, but with no comprehension, and forty years later I feel the same about that comparatively uneventful dream, wherein large and craggy Western forms are glimpsed above a New Jersey farm's horizon. If anyone were to take the first and last syllables of that strange word "Catica," and connect them with the manure-house, I should not thank him for it; a sixteen-year-old boy who has grown up on a farm takes the manure-house for granted, and I did not know the word *caca* at that age.

Perhaps the old dream still resounds for me (the greatest force is in the words of it) because it was simple and soluble and yet escaped me; by which I mean that my waking mind never came to share it. A similar dream, a bit more than a decade later, was understood at once, enjoyed, and put away amongst fathomed experiences. At that time I was busy in left-wing politics, and not long before the dream had helped a young woman gather a great quantity of articles which were to be auctioned for the benefit of a radical organization. One item was a mantilla, which the young woman tried on, and which rather became her. The organization, by the way, was ostensibly concerned with relief for anti-Franco exiles and the like. A short time after the auction, during a house party at Wellfleet, I behaved somewhat improperly toward the young woman, and afterward did not feel easy about it. The dream which summed all this up had no visual content which I can remember; what it amounted to was a resonant voice which intoned, just as I was waking up, "The Spanish Cape Mystery!" There was a mystery novel of that title knocking around our apartment at the time; the author, I believe, was Ellery Queen. It will be seen, however, that the title served, within my dream, to recall the Spanish Civil War, the mantilla, the furtiveness of "front group" politics, Cape Cod, and such guilt as I felt about the girl. Its effect was to remind me of something in a veiled manner; at the same time, the reminder was so tricky and portentous as to amount to a recommendation that something be recognized and then laughed off.

One more dream, which seems to me both hilarious and embarrassing, because I cannot bear self-pity or feelings of nobility in myself. This dream occurred at a time when I had been, as they say, "pressing myself very hard," and apparently felt that I was neglecting my own work or pleasure for the sake of others. In the dream I was standing in a highway some distance from a little town. A steamroller, driven by myself, came toward me as I stood there, and my spirit therefore prudently flew up and looked down on the goings-on. When the steamroller had passed over my body, it lay in the road like a rolled-out ginger cookie; it was not, however, light-brown in color, as gingerbread men are, but was full of red and blue traceries resembling the representations of innards in medical books. Whereupon, like a piece of wrapping paper driven by a gale, my body was peeled from the road surface and whipped across intervening fields to the village, where it at once became a stained-glass window in a church. I believe that this dream requires no explanation, but I report it because, though emotionally disgraceful, it is visually clever and delightful.

Walking to Sleep

As a queen sits down, knowing that a chair will be there,
Or a general raises his hand and is given the field-glasses,
Step off assuredly into the blank of your mind.
Something will come to you. Although at first
You nod through nothing like a fogbound prow,
Gravel will breed in the margins of your gaze,
Perhaps with tussocks or a dusty flower,
And, humped like dolphins playing in the bow-wave,
Hills will suggest themselves. All such suggestions
Are yours to take or leave, but hear this warning:
Let them not be too velvet green, the fields
Which the deft needle of your eye appoints,
Nor the old farm past which you make your way
Too shady-linteled, too instinct with home.
It is precisely from Potemkin barns
With their fresh-painted hex signs on the gables,
Their sparkling gloom within, their stanchion-rattle
And sweet breath of silage, that there comes
The trotting cat whose head is but a skull.
Try to remember this: what you project
Is what you will perceive; what you perceive
With any passion, be it love or terror,
May take on whims and powers of its own.
Therefore a numb and grudging circumspection

Will serve you best, unless you overdo it,
Watching your step too narrowly, refusing
To specify a world, shrinking your purview
To a tight vision of your inching shoes—
Which may, as soon you come to think, be crossing
An unseen gorge upon a rotten trestle.
What you must manage is to bring to mind
A landscape not worth looking at, some bleak
Champaign at dead November's end, its grass
As dry as lichen, and its lichens grey,
Such glumly simple country that a glance
Of flat indifference from time to time
Will stabilize it. Lifeless thus, and leafless,
The view should set at rest all thoughts of ambush.
Nevertheless, permit no roadside thickets
Which, as you pass, might shake with worse than wind;
Revoke all trees and other cover; blast
The upstart boulder which a flicking shape
Has stepped behind; above all, put a stop
To the known stranger up ahead, whose face
Half turns to mark you with a creased expression.
Here let me interject that steady trudging
Can make you drowsy, so that without transition,
As when an old film jumps in the projector,
You will be wading a dun hallway, rounding
A newel post, and starting up the stairs.
Should that occur, adjust to circumstances
And carry on, taking these few precautions:
Detach some portion of your thought to guard
The outside of the building; as you wind
From room to room, leave nothing at your back,
But slough all memories at every threshold;
Nor must you dream of opening any door
Until you have foreseen what lies beyond it.
Regardless of its seeming size, or what
May first impress you as its style or function,
The abrupt structure which involves you now

Will improvise like vapor. Groping down
The gritty cellar steps and past the fuse-box,
Brushing through sheeted lawn-chairs, you emerge
In some cathedral's pillared crypt, and thence,
Your brow alight with carbide, pick your way
To the main shaft through drifts and rubbly tunnels.
Promptly the hoist, ascending toward the pit-head,
Rolls downward past your gaze a dinted rock-face
Peppered with hacks and drill-holes, which acquire
Insensibly the look of hieroglyphics.
Whether to surface now within the vast
Stone tent where Cheops lay secure, or take
The proffered shed of corrugated iron
Which gives at once upon a vacant barracks,
Is up to you. Need I, at this point, tell you
What to avoid? Avoid the pleasant room
Where someone, smiling to herself, has placed
A bowl of yellow freesias. Do not let
The thought of her in yellow, lithe and sleek
As lemonwood, mislead you where the curtains,
Romping like spinnakers which taste the wind,
Bellying out and lifting till the sill
Has shipped a drench of sunlight, then subsiding,
Both warm and cool the love-bed. Your concern
Is not to be detained by dread, or by
Such dear acceptances as would entail it,
But to pursue an ever-dimming course
Of pure transition, treading as in water
Past crumbling tufa, down cloacal halls
Of boarded-up hotels, through attics full
Of glassy taxidermy, moping on
Like a drugged fire-inspector. What you hope for
Is that at some point of the pointless journey,
Indoors or out, and when you least expect it,
Right in the middle of your stride, like that,
So neatly that you never feel a thing,
The kind assassin Sleep will draw a bead
And blow your brains out.

What, are you still awake?
Then you must risk another tack and footing.
Forget what I have said. Open your eyes
To the good blackness not of your room alone
But of the sky you trust is over it,
Whose stars, though foundering in the time to come,
Bequeath us constantly a jetsam beauty.
Now with your knuckles rub your eyelids, seeing
The phosphenes caper like St. Elmo's fire,
And let your head heel over on the pillow
Like a flung skiff on wild Gennesaret.
Let all things storm your thought with the moiled flocking
Of startled rookeries, or flak in air,
Or blossom-fall, and out of that come striding
In the strong dream by which you have been chosen.
Are you upon the roads again? If so,
Be led past honeyed meadows which might tempt
A wolf to graze, and groves which are not you
But answer to your suppler self, that nature
Able to bear the thrush's quirky glee
In stands of chuted light, yet praise as well,
All leaves aside, the barren bark of winter.
When, as you may, you find yourself approaching
A crossroads and its laden gallows tree,
Do not with hooded eyes allow the shadow
Of a man moored in air to bruise your forehead,
But lift your gaze and stare your brother down,
Though the swart crows have pecked his sockets hollow.
As for what turn your travels then will take,
I cannot guess. Long errantry perhaps
Will arm you to be gentle, or the claws
Of nightmare flap you pathless God knows where,
As the crow flies, to meet your dearest horror.
Still, if you are in luck, you may be granted,
As, inland, one can sometimes smell the sea,
A moment's perfect carelessness, in which

To stumble a few steps and sink to sleep
In the same clearing where, in the old story,
A holy man discovered Vishnu sleeping,
Wrapped in his maya, dreaming by a pool
On whose calm face all images whatever
Lay clear, unfathomed, taken as they came.

ROBLEY WILSON

For many years Robley Wilson has edited the venerable *North American Review* while teaching literature and creative writing at the University of Northern Iowa. His first volume of poetry, *Kingdoms of the Ordinary*, won the Agnes Lynch Starrett Prize; his second, *A Pleasure Tree*, won the Society of Midland Authors Poetry Prize. He has also published several volumes of fiction, including the Drue Heinz Prize–winning story collection *Dancing for Men*, and the 1991 novel *The Victim's Daughter*.

A RESOURCE OF DREAMING

All poems—all *serious* poems, I mean—must come somehow out of dreams. "I taste a liquor never brewed," or "Wake, for the sun who scattered into flight / the stars before him from the field of night / drives night away with them," or "My head aches, and a drowsy numbness pains / my sense," or "Once upon a midnight dreary, / while I pondered weak and weary / over many a volume of forgotten lore"—all these come from a universe that lies light-years distant from the waking world. That place is the one e. e. cummings invited us to when he wrote:

> Listen.
> There's a hell of a good universe
> next door.
> Let's go.

It's not quite five A.M. as I start these notes, and I have just waked from a dream, or dreams, already forgotten—lost, as most dreams are, before they can be captured to the page. What was left was the whisper of the lines I've begun with—I don't vouch for their exactness: they are as my groggy memory recalls them, and what genuine dreamer would trouble to look them up?

By now I'm fully awake—the morning paper has this moment arrived on my driveway with the noise of the deliverer's automobile—and the impulse that drove my first paragraph is long gone. The coffee is ready. What follows will be merely work, the advice of my dreams all silent.

When I refer to "serious" poems, I don't have in mind the variations on the mundane which provide the subject matter of much of what passes today for poetry. Interpretation of daily life won't suffice: a poem is the mundane transmuted, art an alchemy of fact, the least figure of the senses formed into magic—like the opening intimation of Keats's nightingale. The trouble is that the universe of dreams is so vast, so *awful* in the root sense of that adjective, that for a writer to offer any single poem as clue to its vastness is to presume too much. The poem below is a small corner of my own dreamworld, a good bit of its magic eroded by the morning after. The residue of the dream—one dream, which I divided into three for reasons of bookkeeping—is the best of the poem, especially the last line of it.

Dream and poem grew out of a student picnic, held beside a river—the Cedar, in Iowa—in front of a house that at one time had belonged to a university colleague. What I most remember of that picnic, more than twenty years after the fact, is the discomfort of feeling out of place among men and women half my age. (That's always good for a poem, that out-of-placeness, even without sleep or hypnagogy.)

The dream simply made the picnic, its guests and its setting, into a chronology of illusions. The opening turns the water's real pollution into something ominously defeating. The poem's second section becomes, at that remove, more problematic (the bottles are the beer the picnickers drank, but what prompted the dead kittens? I wonder) and is nearly a tract on saving the environment. Section 3 resolves despair by producing—what? An angel, a muse, a faceless "you" surely inspired by a married student at the real event. Today I recall that it was a Fourth of July picnic; there were fireworks that must in my dream have murdered fish and kittens.

As for the two children, they may have been actual, or they may have been versions of my own two sons; they may even have been fore-shadows of the two daughters I inherited years later when I remarried. In any case, they seem in the poem to stand for love and nurture and rebirth, and they lead to the poem's statement of what might be called "mystical optimism."

Three Dreams

1.

I am walking along a sandy shore
by myself, looking into the lake;
in its brown depths I begin to see
fish, all sizes. I feel pleasure
at first, and then dismay, for all
of them float motionless, rigid,
all dead just under the surface.

2.

A place to recover. But my ease
in the cool shade of the birches,
my joy in the small white flowers
underfoot—these vanish in a moment:
the ground is all at once bare, cans
and green bottles litter the woods.
I find myself at the brink of a pit.

Now I am looking down on the colors
of a different death—browns, yellows,
grays and blacks, whites and oranges.
This is a grave of kittens; they are
stacked like firewood, they have not
begun to decay, they are the pets
of a hundred children who mourn them.

3.

Then you appear, magically, a child
holding each of your hands; a smile
begins when you see me. I meet you,
I say: Come witness these horrible,
horrible things. I show you the fish.
As we watch, they flex, turn upright
and swim away in the dark water.

I take you to the kittens' graveyard,
and of course you and your children
kneel at the edge to pick up, one
by one, the tiny, squirming animals;
I hear them mewing, hear the laughter
of your children. You say to me:
You must expect things to be changed.

What I've said about the poem's imagery is only an accounting,
not an interpretation (which, in any case, would be beyond my powers).
In its early drafts the poem was more than twice as long; probably it is still
longer than it needs to be. That last line—I can hear those dreamwords
in my head even now.

SELECTED BIBLIOGRAPHY

Alvarez, A. *Night: An Exploration of Night Life, Night Language, Sleep, and Dreams*. New York: Norton, 1995.

Bachelard, Gaston. *The Poetics of Reverie*. Translated by Daniel Russell. New York: Orion, 1969.

———. *The Poetics of Space*. Translated by Maria Jolas. Boston: Beacon Press, 1969.

———. *The Psychoanalysis of Fire*. Translated by Alan C. M. Ross. Boston: Beacon Press, 1964.

Benedikt, Michael, ed. *The Poetry of Surrealism*. Boston: Little, Brown, 1974.

Brook, Stephen. *The Oxford Book of Dreams*. New York and Oxford: Oxford University Press, 1983.

Bush, Ronald. *T. S. Eliot: A Study in Character and Style*. New York and Oxford: Oxford University Press, 1983.

Epel, Naomi, ed. *Writers Dreaming*. New York: Crown, 1993.

Freud, Sigmund. *The Interpretation of Dreams*. Translated by James Strachey. New York: Basic Books, 1971.

Gardner, Helen. *The Composition of Four Quartets*. New York and Oxford: Oxford University Press, 1978.

Hillman, James. *The Dream and the Underworld*. New York: Harper and Row, 1979.

Hooker, Joan Fillmore. *T. S. Eliot's Poems in French Translation: Pierre Leyris and Others*. Ann Arbor, Mich.: UMI Research Press, 1983.

Hudson, Liam. *Night Life: The Interpretation of Dreams*. New York: St. Martin's Press, 1985.

Jones, Richard M. *The Dream Poet*. Cambridge, Mass.: Schenkman, 1979.

Jung, Carl G. *The Portable Jung*. Edited by Joseph Campbell. New York: Viking Penguin, 1971.

Kuusisto, Stephen, Deborah Tall, and David Weiss, eds. *The Poet's Notebook: Excerpts from the Notebooks of Twenty-Six American Poets*. New York: Norton, 1995.

Lewis, James R. *The Dream Encyclopedia*. Detroit and Washington: Visible Ink Press, 1995.

Lippard, Lucy R., ed. *Surrealists on Art*. Englewood Cliffs, N.J.: Prentice-Hall, 1970.

Mariani, Paul. *Dream Song: The Life of John Berryman*. New York: William Morrow, 1990.

———. *Lost Puritan: A Life of Robert Lowell*. New York: Norton, 1994.

———. *William Carlos Williams: A New World Naked*. New York: McGraw-Hill, 1981.

Middlebrook, Diane Wood. *Anne Sexton: A Biography*. Boston: Houghton Mifflin, 1991.

Moffett, Judith. *James Merrill: An Introduction to the Poetry*. New York: Columbia University Press, 1984.

Roheim, Geza. *The Gates of the Dream*. New York: International Universities Press, 1952.

Rothenberg, Albert. *The Emerging Goddess: The Creative Process in Art, Science, and Other Fields*. Chicago: University of Chicago Press, 1979.

Rycroft, Charles. *The Innocence of Dreams*. New York: Pantheon, 1979.

Townley, Roderick. *The Early Poetry of William Carlos Williams*. Ithaca and London: Cornell University Press, 1975.

Ullman, Montague, and Claire Limmer. *The Variety of Dream Experience: Expanding Our Ways of Working with Dreams*. New York: Continuum, 1987.

Yenser, Stephen. *The Consuming Myth: The Work of James Merrill*. Cambridge, Mass.: Harvard University Press, 1987.

The following poems or essays are reprinted with permission of the publishers.

Laurel Blossom's poems "Now We Are 48" and "No Is the Answer, the Answer Is No," in *The Papers Said* (Santa Cruz: Greenhouse Review Press, 1993); her poems "Doomed" and "The Spin of the Earth," in *What's Wrong* (Cleveland: The Rowfant Club, 1987).

Nicholas Christopher's poems "After a Long Illness," "The Anonymous Letter," "The Lights of Siena as Seen from Florence in a Dream," and "Outside Perpignan in Heavy Rain" reprinted with permission of the author.

Sarah Cotterill's poem "Coming of the Dam," from *In the Nocturnal Animal House* (West Lafayette, Ind.: Purdue University Press, 1991).

Rachel Hadas's poems "May" and "Tea and a Dream," in *Verse* 13, no. 1 (1996); and "Around Lake Erie and Across the Hudson," in *Literary Cavalcade* 50, no. 1 (Sept. 1997).

Anthony Hecht's poem "Clair de Lune," in *Collected Earlier Poems* (New York: Knopf, 1990).

Edward Hirsch's poem "For the Sleepwalkers," in *For the Sleepwalkers* (New York: Knopf, 1981); his poem, "I Need Help," in *Wild Gratitude* (New York: Knopf, 1985).

John Hollander's essay, "The Dream of the Trumpeter," first published in *DreamWorks* 1, no. 2 (summer 1980).

David Ignatow's poem "The Bagel," in *Against the Evidence: Selected Poems 1934–1994* (Middletown, Conn.: Wesleyan University Press, 1995).

Maxine Kumin's essay, "Scrubbed Up and Sent to School," published as "Dreaming in Poetry" in *Michigan Quarterly Review* (winter 1997).

Denise Levertov's essay, "Interweavings: Reflections on the Role of Dream in the Making of Poems," from *Light Up the Cave* (New York: New Directions, 1981).

Philip Levine's poem "They Feed They Lion," from *New Selected Poems* (New York: Knopf, 1991).

Gerard Malanga's poem "Morning of January 2, 1993," published with permission of the author.

Paul Mariani's poems "What the Wind Said" and "Ghost," from *The Great Wheel* (New York: Norton, 1997); his poem "Salvage Operations," in *Salvage Operations: Selected Poems* (New York: Norton, 1990).

J. D. McClatchy's essay, "Some Footnotes to My Dreams," first published as "Dreaming" in his collection, *Twenty Questions* (New York: Columbia University Press, 1998).

Wesley McNair's poem "A Dream of Herman," in *The Faces of Americans in 1853* (Columbia, Mo.: University of Missouri Press, 1983); his poems "After My Stepfather's Death" and "The Abandonment," in *The Town of No and My Brother Running* (Boston: Godine, 1997).

Joyce Carol Oates's poems "Nostalgia" and "The Lord Is My Shepherd, I Shall Not Want," reprinted with permission from Ontario Review Press, Princeton, New Jersey.

David Ray's poem "The Return," from *Sam's Book* (Middletown, Conn.: Wesleyan University Press, 1987).

Diane Wakoski's poems "Coins & Coffins," "Possession Poem," and "Justice Is Reason

Enough" in *Emerald Ice: Selected Poems, 1962–1987* (Santa Rosa, Calif.: Black Sparrow, 1988).

Jane O. Wayne's poem "Tooth and Nail" reprinted with permission of the author; her poem "Your Recurring Dream," from *A Strange Heart* (Kansas City: Helicon Nine Editions, 1996).

Theodore Weiss's poem "Caliban Remembers," from *Selected Poems* (Evanston, Ill.: TriQuarterly Books, 1995).

Richard Wilbur's essay, "A Note on Poetry and Dreams," published in different form as "Movies and Dreams" in *The Catbird's Song: Prose Pieces, 1963–1995* (New York: Harcourt Brace, 1997); his poem "Walking to Sleep," from *New and Collected Poems* (New York: Harcourt Brace Jovanovich, 1988).

Robley Wilson's poem "Three Dreams," from *Kingdoms of the Ordinary* (Pittsburgh, Pa.: University of Pittsburgh Press, 1987).

Library of Congress Cataloging-in-Publication Data

Night errands : how poets use dreams / edited by Roderick Townley.
   p. cm.
   Includes bibliographical references (p.   ) and index.
   ISBN 0-8229-4077-9 (acid-free paper)
   1. American poetry—20th century—History and criticism—Theory, etc. 2. Dreams in literature. 3. Poetry—Authorship. I. Townley, Roderick, 1942–
   PS310.D74 N54 1998
   811'.509353—ddc21

                                        98-19748